A Parley with Youth

A Parley with Youth

*Dialogues With High School
Students About Virtue*

Joshua Gibbs

CiRCE
Concord, NC

Published in the USA
by the CiRCE Institute
© 2024 Joshua Gibbs

ISBN: 979-8-9869172-9-0

All rights reserved. This publication may not be reproduced, stored in a retrieval system, or transmitted, in any form or by any means, without the prior written permission of the CiRCE Institute.

For information:
CiRCE Institute
6125 Lumber Lane
Kannapolis, NC 28083
www.circeinstitute.com

Cover design by Graeme Pitman

For my father, who gave a damn.

Table of Contents

Introduction - i

Dialogue 1: On Magic - 1

Dialogue 2: On Friendship & Family - 11

Dialogue 3: On Video Games - 51

Dialogue 4: On Disagreeing with Your Church - 69

Dialogue 5: On Good Taste - 83

Dialogue 6: On College - 117

Dialogue 7: Lead Me into Temptation - 137

Dialogue 8: On Dating in High School - 149

Dialogue 9: On Optimism & Identity - 161

Dialogue 10: On Learning - 187

Dialogue 11: On Finding Your Voice - 199

Dialogue 12: On Loopholes - 211

Dialogue 13: On Secrets - 223

Introduction

AS A HIGH SCHOOL TEACHER, a good portion of my life has been spent in the presence of teenagers. Five days a week, nine months a year, for sixteen years now, I have stood in front of rooms full of teenagers and talked with them. I have listened to them talk about themselves and observed them, and so I know that they do not entirely understand themselves. When they read novels, they think they want characters they can relate to. They think they want adults to take their tastes and preferences seriously. They think they will be happy when they have a little more freedom. They think they could endure any sort of suffering with patience if only someone—a girlfriend, a boyfriend—would vindicate their existence by voluntarily showing them preference and love. They think they will pray more when they grow up and leave home. In reality, none of these things is true.

Strangely enough, teenagers have learned to believe such things about themselves from adults—adults who do not understand teenagers but pretend to. In order to understand teenagers, three conditions are needful. First, one must no longer be a teenager. Second, one must love teenagers. And third, one must remember his own teenage years with great clarity.

I believe the first two conditions necessarily go together. Love must be directed outside the self, away from the self, and until a man has fully set his own youth in the past, he cannot love youth as his other. It is for this reason that people in their early twenties often do a miserable job managing large groups of teenagers. I have witnessed this many times during retreats at camps wherein small crews of college students are given the task of organizing games for high school students or policing free time by the lake. Twentysomething camp counselors have a tendency to mask their discomfort with authority by speaking to teenagers in a sort of condescending, sing-songy tone and by giving needlessly simple instructions on how to do banal tasks. While teenagers are prone to think that twentysomethings will make for lenient judges, generous masters, and understanding partners, the average twentysomething overseeing a game of high school dodgeball explains the rules like a demeaning drill sergeant, then stands in the corner joking with his twentysomething friends while the game falls apart. There is a case to be made that one's teenage years don't really end until twenty-seven, the age when most people begin rediscovering their parents.

The most demanding part of understanding teenagers is remembering your own teenage years clearly. In order to do this, one must have teenage years that are worth remembering—worth retelling—but also an ability to interpret the deeper meaning of mere autobiographical data. The sort of man who has few stories to tell about high school, or who insists that high school was the worst period of his life, or who simply spent his teens trying to get good grades and be left alone—this man is not the stuff great high school teachers are made of. At the age of forty, a good high school teacher should have recently watched whatever his favorite film was back when he was sixteen. He should still occasionally listen to his favorite records from high school. The pleasure of hearing these records should be quite different twenty-five years later, but he should spend time remembering the pleasure he took from them in his youth. It is only by psychologically and emotionally tracing his own path back to youth that a teacher can trace a path forward to maturity for his students.

All this to say, there was probably no better line of work for a person as nostalgic as myself than teaching high school literature.

There was a learning curve, of course. I was only twenty-four when I taught my first class. I referred to my students as "you guys" and believed I could win their favor by making numerous allusions to popular culture. Four years later, I was still dressing to impress my students, but my second child had just been born and I had begun growing the beard which I have worn ever since. What is more, it was this same year that two disgruntled parents came after my job, and I experienced for the first time what it was like to have actual enemies. Around this time, I began paying closer attention to the way other adults spoke to teenagers and about teenagers. Christians had begun noticing just how many children raised in Christian households summarily abandoned the faith in college. I also noticed the ease with which parents brushed off criticism of their children, the blithe and blind optimism that regarded insolent students as "basically good kids," and the rising evangelical insistence that praise was the only sort of encouragement safe to give anyone, especially teenagers.

When I reflected on my own youth, though, some of the most important conversations I had with adults were brief, particular, and pointed. Two primarily stood out in my memory.

At the age of nineteen or twenty, I was leaving the house one day just as my father was coming home, and as I waved to him, he motioned for me to stop. He asked me where I was going, and I said I was on my way to spend time with some friends. "Are there going to be girls there?" he asked. I said there would be. "You need to dress like you give a damn," he said. In fact, the clothes I was wearing had just been pulled from a pile of wrinkled laundry on the floor. Up to that moment, it was one of just two times I had ever heard my father curse. I went back in, ironed my shirt, ironed my pants, and have been rather faithful to wear presentable clothes in public ever since.

Another occasion from my youth I recalled was from the period of my engagement. Having been raised in a Reformed community wherein feasting played an important role in public life, nearly every wedding reception I had ever attended was replete with drinking and dancing. It was a point of honor. However, my wife's parents did not drink, and my wife's grandfather was a teetotaler who positively despised alcohol, and so I was caught between wanting to give my friends the sort of reception they were accustomed to and offending my wife's family the second I became a part of it. For weeks, the issue revolved in my mind. I went to older men in my church and presented the case to them, but their constant refrain was, "This is a wisdom issue," after which they presented me with my various options and what taking each of the options would cost me. I already knew all this, though. I knew it was a wisdom issue. The problem was that I was young, dumb, had no wisdom, and no one seemed willing to part with any of theirs. Finally, I asked the pastor of a different church. Before asking, I said, "Tell me what to do. Whatever you tell me to do, I'll do, because I have tired of trying to sort the issue out for myself." After explaining the conundrum to him, he asked, "Who is paying for the wedding?" I told him my in-laws were paying for it. "If they're paying, it's their call," he said, and that was that. The decision was made. I slept easy again and did not regret my decision.

Of course, there were other stories of bracing, effective adult advice I could recall from my youth, but they were all types of these two: the first was perfectly unsentimental, the second unapologetically certain. And yet the sort of advice I saw most adults offering teenagers was generic, vague, and entirely bereft of any exhortation to mature habits of life. When adults pray for groups of teenagers, they often conclude by asking God to "help everyone have fun," as though having fun were a really important task that requires divine assistance. When advising teenagers on spiritual problems, adults tend toward clichés about "loving God more" or "having more faith," but shy away from telling students to throw their video game consoles away and quit social media. Worse still, many Christian adults have given themselves over entirely to the psychologization of sin, especially when dealing with their own children. Cowardice is "a fear of failure." Pride "doesn't respond well to criticism." Nearly any personality quirk or idiosyncrasy, no matter how destructive or debilitating, is the morally neutral result of being introverted, extroverted, or stressed. Even Republican parents who otherwise complain about safe spaces, snowflakes, and welfare bristle at the word "punishment," insist on "consequences," and often argue that their own children should not receive consequences but "grace" whenever they break the rules.

My strategy for talking with high school students about their temptations, problems, hopes, and fears has slowly emerged while talking with their parents over the last decade. What do all those parents have in common who raise happy, obedient, productive children who keep the faith after they leave home? And what do all those parents have in common whose children quickly give up on church as soon as they go off to college? What do all those teachers have in common whose students become their friends after graduation? And what about all those teachers whose former students never return for a chat? Considering these questions has persuaded me to push my students to recognize all the special exceptions they have granted themselves and how their suffering usually emerges from the fact they think themselves unique. Most of the dialogues in this collection aim to bring students to this realization.

There is a sense in which all the dialogues in this book are fictional, and yet I have also had these sorts of conversations with sophomores and juniors more times than I can count. Like adults, teenagers like to talk about the same things over and over again. When I was in high school, we felt very sophisticated when talking about the legalization of marijuana. The modern teenager feels quite grown up when talking about disorders and therapies. They have a passing interest in news headlines, but they are always game for a discussion of romance. While their boldest assertions are typically reserved for sports, teenagers are at their most genuinely philosophical when talking about friendship. Adults often believe that teenagers need help having a good time, but what teenagers want most is to dress themselves and listen to their own music with their own friends. They are vexed when adults dictate any of these three things. While teenagers tend to believe they are always right—because, as Aristotle notes, their ideas have never been tested—Christian teenagers also tend to think too highly of adults and to believe themselves more responsible for all the suffering in the world than is fair. At the same time, teenagers are often quite horrified when they learn that many adults still struggle with the same sins that beset them in high school, for most teenagers believe they will naturally become good and responsible as soon as they marry. Many teenagers live in constant fear of being discovered, caught, or found out—actually, this is true not just of teenagers but of all people—and yet, the fear is new to teenagers because they have very little experience with hiding things and keeping secrets.

While they believe they will be good as soon as they become adults, most Christian teenagers are willing to admit they sin more this year than last, and that they sinned more last year than the year before, and the same is true of every year going all the way back to the age of seven or eight. When you point this out to a roomful of teenagers, they are dumbfounded, for most have secretly known this for quite some time and are surprised to see all their peers soberly agree. Reader, whether you are a youth group leader, a pastor, a priest, a parent, or a teacher, know that on whatever occasion you decide to point this out to the high school students you shepherd, you will have the room's undivided attention and respect in whatever you say next.

Some of what I know about talking to teenagers comes from trial and error. They are surprisingly unmoved by heartfelt appeals to popular culture, even though they desperately love popular culture. They know when they are being flattered and rarely mind when an adult tells them their taste in music is juvenile, for most Christian teenagers secretly know they cannot take their childish preferences into motherhood or fatherhood. When adulthood is presented as something genuinely other than adolescence, teenagers are relieved, for they both want and know this to be true.

The purpose of this book is to give adults persuasive, philosophically sound, and psychologically realistic examples of talking with high school students. Ours is a sentimental age, which means we are typically terrified of giving bad news or painful critiques (in person, at least), although the backlash against this sentimentality also prompts some to contrarianism, and so they believe the only honest form of communication is brazen, defiant, and rude. However, a conversation wherein seeking virtue is the goal does not grant ultimate priority to human feelings, but neither does it dismiss the importance which the heart must play in spiritual contentment. For this reason, a good conversation does not flatter either party, but neither does it senselessly demean the other. Rather, both partners finish the conversation with an accurate estimation of their own merits and responsibilities. St. Paul doesn't command us to "not think" of ourselves, or to "not think highly of ourselves," but to "not think of [ourselves] more highly than we ought," which will allow us to properly assess what service we owe others and what is fair to expect of them in return.

At the same time, this book is a series of dialogues with my students, which is to say that it was also written for a young audience. In the same way men benefit from listening to average, arguably happy women demystify the female mind, or the way the middle-class benefit from having the mind of the rich demystified, or vice versa, I believe teenagers can benefit from having the average adult mind demystified, which is something I aim to do here. They wonder why husbands and wives are not so fond of one another as teenagers are of their crushes—why married people do not hang on one another's words, whether they used to, why they stopped, and whether they mind the change. They wonder why their parents' friends seem to mean so little to them, why their parents are so averse to risk, why they care so little about winning games, and why they talk so often of money. In reading this book, I hope high school students find the idea of becoming adults less distressing, more interesting, and worth laboring for.

DIALOGUE 1
On Magic

Toby: Why do you let your kids read *Harry Potter* books?

Gibbs: Why not?

Toby: St. Augustine would not have let his kids read books which made wizards out to be heroes. He would have burned those books just like the Ephesian Christians burned their books of magic in Acts 19.

Gibbs: Finally! A good argument against the *Harry Potter* series.

Toby: What do you mean, "Finally"?

Gibbs: Most arguments against *Harry Potter* books are quite awful. I've heard people speak as though children who read *The Prisoner of Azkaban* are going to start sacrificing their pets to the devil, which is obviously absurd. But you're right. St. Augustine would certainly not have let his son read *The Sorcerer's Stone*. He would have pitched it straight into the flames. You will get no argument from me on that point.

Toby: You are normally not one to disagree with St. Augustine.

Gibbs: Well, I don't disagree with him on this one.

Toby: What do you mean?

Gibbs: St. Augustine lived in a time when the average man who owned books of magic had also sacrificed a few animals to demons. In St. Augustine's day, animal sacrifice had been lately outlawed by the Roman government, although a stalwart remnant of pagans lived on who probably tried to please the gods in secret.

Toby: What do animal sacrifices have to do with the *Harry Potter* series?

Gibbs: The argument you gave against the *Harry Potter* series was entirely based on ancient and late antique perceptions of magic. At that time, magic was inextricably tied to pagan cosmology, but that is simply not true anymore. The kind of person who owned books of magic in the fourth century is nothing like the kind of person who owns books that reference magic today. Simply put, owning a *Harry Potter* book today is not a sign of allegiance with the devil.

Toby: Why not?

Gibbs: Because the devil does not care about magic anymore, at least not where you and I live. He is far more interested in convincing people that neither magic nor miracles is possible. For that reason, I imagine the devil is even more opposed to the *Harry Potter* books than you are.

Toby: I doubt that. I am quite opposed to those books.

Gibbs: How come?

Toby: Because witchcraft is a sin and those books make witchcraft out to be virtuous. What is evil, those books call "good."

Gibbs: What is "witchcraft"?

Toby: The practice of magic.

Gibbs: And what is magic?

Toby: The invocation of demonic power.

Gibbs: Is that really the way the word "magic" is used today?

Toby: If not, then the devil has hidden behind a casual usage of the word.

Gibbs: So, when a young woman says, "We danced, then he kissed me for the first time. It was magical," the devil is hiding behind her words?

Toby: No, in that case, she is using the word as a metaphor.

Gibbs: And why did we determine that magic was a fitting metaphor for romance?

Toby: We have forgotten God.

Gibbs: What does the young woman mean when she says the kiss was "magical"?

Toby: She means the kiss felt like something beyond this world, unconstrained by the normal rules of reality.

Gibbs: Very good. And don't you ever encounter such things as well—things which seem to come from beyond this world? Things unconstrained by the normal rules of reality?

Toby: Nothing comes to mind.

Gibbs: How lamentable! Nothing?

Toby: No. But I don't see why that is lamentable.

Gibbs: You've never been charmed by a lovely song or enchanted by the beauty of a woman?

Toby: No. That's simply not how I would describe it—at least, not anymore.

Gibbs: Are you as offended by "charming" songs and "enchanting" women as you are by the magic in *Harry Potter* books?

ON MAGIC

Toby: I will admit, I never connected "charming" things and "enchanting" things to their magical roots before.

Gibbs: Why not?

Toby: Those words are simply too common.

Gibbs: But also because nobody in the world references "charming" things or "enchanting" things with an eye toward worshipping the devil. These words meant something very different in a former age, but their meaning has quite changed.

Toby: These words retain at least some of their former meaning, though.

Gibbs: Of course, which is why we still use them.

Toby: And in retaining some of their former meaning, these words are still impious.

Gibbs: Magic has pagan roots. You will get no argument from me there. Should Christians abstain from absolutely everything with pagan roots?

Toby: Like what?

Gibbs: Are you opposed to the Olympic Games?

Toby: Of course not.

Gibbs: Despite the fact the Olympic Games were originally held in honor of Zeus?

Toby: The modern Olympic Games are not held in honor of Zeus.

Gibbs: Modern references to magic do not honor Zeus either. Zeus is no more present in the modern Olympics than he is in *The Sorcerer's Stone*. Are you opposed to theaters? Plays? You are aware, of course, that the Christian emperor Theodosius closed down the Olympic games and shuttered all theaters and playhouses back in the fourth century because he determined they were inextricably bound up with the worship of the gods?

Toby: That is all well and good, but absolutely no one in the Olympics today runs for the glory of Zeus.

Gibbs: Agreed. The meaning of the Olympics has changed.

Toby: I see your point, but modern magic still involves spells and potions and incantations.

Gibbs: And the modern relay still involves runners and batons and a large oval course. I find it mind-boggling that you are trying to connect the magic performed in the *Harry Potter* series with the magic performed by ancient pagans. It seems you know nothing of ancient magic whatsoever, which was a vulgar, bloody, brutal, heartless, enslaving art, not the kind of thing happy children would play for an afternoon before skipping in for supper.

Toby: The fact that children can play a thing happily does not mean that thing is good. The heart is deceitfully wicked, and we are all born at enmity with God.

Gibbs: Just a moment ago, the fact a bunch of children could happily run a relay race without a thought of Zeus was sufficient proof the Olympic games were no longer demonic.

Toby: Well, perhaps the Olympics are demonic, as well.

Gibbs: Are tragedies demonic, too? The word tragedy means "goat song," after all, a reference to the animal sacrificed to Dionysus before Greek plays, which were all performed in his honor. Must we do away with the theater, as well? No more films? No more *Hamlet*?

Toby: You have a very fine slippery slope argument going, but I am not persuaded. You're trying to convince me that just because we cannot root out everything pagan from our society, we should not lift a finger to remove anything pagan. I am simply arguing that not giving children *Harry Potter* books is quite easy, and that by not exposing your children to magic, you honor your Christian forebears who believed magic was a great blight upon creation.

Gibbs: In his biography of St. Francis of Assisi, Chesterton suggested that the Middle Ages were a thousand-year long period of fasting, which was necessary because so much of human life had been tainted by the demonic. In other words, the dullness and dreariness of the Middle Ages was Lenten, like Christ forsaking the good things of the world to prepare in the wilderness for His temptation by the devil. After a thousand years, though, all the things which had formerly been stained by malign spiritual powers had been cleansed of those stains, and men were free to enjoy them again in good conscience. Of all the institutions and things stained by demons, Chesterton argued, the earth itself was the greatest victim, because demons had hijacked the goodness of nature for thousands of years before Christ. Demons had stolen the gifts of God and held them for ransom. Demons had distorted nature and corrupted man's understanding and proper love of nature. Christ came to reclaim the world, but the reclamation would take some time.

Toby: Can we not be grateful for nature without invoking the worship of demons? Can sunsets not simply be "beautiful"? Why must they be "magical"?

Gibbs: In ancient times, magic was the bondage of nature to the god of this world, the devil. But in these latter days, magic is the restoration of wonder and thanks for nature. Magic, enchantment, charm, spellbinding things, entrancing things—this is the language we use to describe natural things which are suddenly illumined by supernatural glory and transcendent beauty. In Christian societies like ours, magic is very rarely practiced. It is far more of a way of viewing the world with awe. The *Harry Potter* series isn't conning children into consorting with demons. Those books are restoring children's delight in school after the materialists and secularists turned schools into godless factories. Magic is now a weapon of joy for fighting Darwin, Dewey, and all the other "prophets of doom" who have lately tried to strip all the wonder from the world. If St. Augustine were alive today, he wouldn't burn *Harry Potter* books. He would burn all the Katy Perry albums and Taylor Swift albums that have cast spells of mind-numbing banality on innocent young girls. He would destroy all the intellectually impoverished cinematic spectacles that have mesmerized and hypnotized our young men.

Toby: You really think so?

Gibbs: There are two kinds of Christians today. One kind thinks the other is too pagan, the other thinks the former is too atheistic. You can guess which kind I am.

Toby: So, you admit your worship of God is tainted by paganism?

Gibbs: Tainted? No. After reflecting on the extreme poverty of imagination which besets disenchanted modern men, C.S. Lewis wrote in "Modern Man and His Categories of Thought," "I sometimes wonder whether we shall not have to re-convert men to real Paganism as a preliminary to converting them to Christianity." I am not much worried that my daughters will end up worshipping Zeus or Jupiter, but I am worried they will end up worshipping their own autonomy, because droves of Christians these days are bewitched by the materialist spirit of our age and do not know otherwise. When Christians fight against magic, they have radically misunderstood where the real threat of this age comes from. But my children will know the world is charmed by Jesus Christ Himself.

DIALOGUE 2

On Friendship & Family

Taylor: I shouldn't name him, but there's a student at this school who is having a rough year. A number of us are really worried about him.

Gibbs: Tell me about him.

Taylor: He started drinking. He gets alcohol from someone on his travel soccer team. He was a good guy until a year ago, but he has hidden everything, so his parents trust him. They trust him entirely too much, though, and he does bad things when they leave for the weekend. He cheats on tests and brags about it. He makes the most awful jokes about the teachers, especially Ms. Davidson. I've asked several adults I trust about what I should do for him.

Gibbs: Who have you spoken to about this?

Taylor: My youth pastor and a friend from church who is in college.

Gibbs: And what have they told you?

Taylor: My youth pastor said we shouldn't give up on him. We should surround him, love him, and have confidence that righteousness is stronger than sin.

Gibbs: That sounds like what youth pastors say. When he said you should "surround him and love him," did he explain what he meant?

Taylor: He said we shouldn't abandon him. We need to be there for him and lift him up.

Gibbs: That is still quite vague.

Taylor: We shouldn't shun him. We should invite him to events and parties. We shouldn't cut him out of the group text. We should still have lunch with him. If he becomes isolated, it will only make him worse.

Gibbs: How will it make him worse?

Taylor: There won't be anyone to keep him accountable.

Gibbs: Are you keeping him accountable now?

Taylor: What do you mean?

Gibbs: Have you confronted him on his sin? Have you told him you want no part in his sin? Have you told his parents what he's doing?

Taylor: You can keep people accountable in other ways.

Gibbs: How are you keeping him accountable?

Taylor: In being around him, we see everything he does. There are witnesses.

Gibbs: What good are witnesses? Based on what you've said, it seems he tells everyone at school about the bad things he does which they aren't around to see. Besides, in a court of law, the only kind of witness that is worth anything is a witness who isn't afraid to testify.

Taylor: But if we tell his parents what he is doing, he won't trust us anymore.

Gibbs: So? Thus far, I am not sure what he needs you for.

Taylor: If we tell his parents, he won't trust us anymore and he'll lash out against his parents. If we shun him, he'll lash out against us. He'll become worse just to win our attention. We need to stay with him. He needs us to help keep him relatively stable.

Gibbs: The idea that he needs you around to remain relatively stable is rather odd given that he has gotten progressively worse for the last year, and all the while you've been around. Your youth pastor suggested you surround him and love him, which sounds a good bit like, "Don't do anything. Just hope things change for the better." If he's gotten worse over the last year while you've surrounded him and loved him, why not admit that your attention is making him worse?

Taylor: There may not be a direct connection, though.

Gibbs: It sounds as though you have several friends who are concerned for this troubled young man as well. How big is the circle of friends who spend time with him, worry about him, and listen to his boasting?

Taylor: Seven or eight, although some are closer to him than others.

Gibbs: In the last year, how many of the seven or eight good kids who are going to "surround him and love him" have joined with him in his sin on a few occasions?

Taylor: I don't think that's a fair question.

Gibbs: Why?

Taylor: Once again, there might not be a direct connection. Everyone falls to temptation sometimes.

Gibbs: So, several of the surrounding, loving crowd have joined him in the drinking and the degrading jokes.

Taylor: Yes, and I see where you're going with this. You see his sin infecting those around him. You think we need to shun him, so the infections do not become worse. But if his problems emerged while he was in a community, then the community needs to help him overcome his problems.

Gibbs: There are several ways for his community to help, though. In what way does "surrounding him and loving him" involve real help? Does anyone who is surrounding him and loving him tell him to stop his foolishness? Does anyone correct him? Confront him?

Taylor: None of us is perfect, though. Who are we to judge?

Gibbs: If you're not able to judge, you're not able to help. We determine other people need help by making some sort of judgment about them and about ourselves as well. I would wager that the seven or eight of you who are going to surround and love this troubled young man have already been a little compromised by his sins. Because of this, you cannot honestly call this guy to repent of his sins without him throwing the call to repent back in your faces. As none of you wants to confess your sins to your parents, neither are you willing to tell this fellow he must own up to his sins. It is a little hard to say whether you really care about this young man or if you're as bad off as he is and simply looking for a way to feel better about yourself. "I have been bad but not as bad as that fellow" is something that fellow says all the time.

Taylor: Look, no one's perfect. You're a teacher, though. You must understand that some people are worse off than others. You worry more about some students than others, even though you have your own sins to confess. If I just wanted to feel better about myself, I would have quit asking adults for advice after my youth pastor gave me an easy way out.

Gibbs: A fair point. Why didn't you stop after your youth pastor gave you an easy way out?

Taylor: I'm not entirely convinced it is the easy way out. On the one hand, it's easier to surround him and love him than to confront him, because he would throw the accusations back in our faces. You're right about that. On the other hand, if we confront him, he will run from us. He needs some good influences in his life. If he doesn't have his friends from school, he won't have any good influences at all.

Gibbs: Describe for me how a good influence works.

Taylor: Do you honestly mean that you've never heard the expression "a good influence" before?

Gibbs: Humor me. Explain to me how it works.

Taylor: People become like their friends. If you have a friend who likes rock music, eventually you will like rock music, too. People absorb the tastes, preferences, and beliefs of their friends. If the people you spend time with have good habits, you will develop good habits as well.

Gibbs: And what are the good habits that you and your friends are hoping to lend to this troubled young man? Do you pray together and read the Scriptures aloud together?

Taylor: It's not what we do. It's more of what we don't do that I hope rubs off. You don't have to drink and curse to have fun.

Gibbs: How many times in your life have you seen good influence rub off?

Taylor: I don't know. But I believe goodness is more powerful than wickedness. If bad influence is possible—and I believe it is because I have seen it—then good influence must be possible as well.

Gibbs: When you say that goodness is more powerful than wickedness, what do you mean?

Taylor: I mean God is stronger than the devil and God's people are stronger than their enemies.

Gibbs: What is the difference between good influence and bad influence?

Taylor: Is it not obvious?

Gibbs: No. Both the idea of "good influence" and "bad influence" presume two parties—one good and one bad. When a "good influence" takes place, the bad takes on the qualities of the good. When a "bad influence" takes place, the good takes on the qualities of the bad. You keep saying that goodness is more powerful than wickedness, which would mean that bad influence is impossible.

Taylor: How do you explain the difference between good influence and bad influence, then?

Gibbs: To begin with, I don't think "good influence" exists—at least not in the way you're using the term.

Taylor: In all your years as a teacher, you've never seen a good student lead a weak student to goodness? You've never seen a weak student grow in strength through the influence of a strong student?

Gibbs: How does spiritual strength manifest itself?

Taylor: In overcoming temptation.

Gibbs: And what is the best way to overcome temptation?

Taylor: With prayer.

Gibbs: I disagree.

Taylor: Are you serious?

Gibbs: Maybe. What sort of prayer do you mean?

Taylor: Prayers for wisdom.

Gibbs: Then, yes, I am serious. If a man is confronted by profound temptations, the last thing he should do is sit down, make himself comfortable, and begin praying for wisdom.

Taylor: What should he do?

Gibbs: Accept the wisdom God has already given you in the Scriptures, in the writings of great saints, and in the chapter on common sense which is written in the book of nature.

Taylor: And what is that wisdom?

Gibbs: Run. Do what Eve should have done. When you get to a safe distance, begin praying that you would not invent specious reasons to go back. When Joseph was tempted to sleep with Potiphar's wife, he didn't pray the temptation would pass.

Taylor: What did he do?

Gibbs: He fled her presence so quickly that he left his garment in her clutched hands. This is Christ's teaching in the Sermon on the Mount, as well. If your right eye causes you to sin, pluck it out. Cut yourself off from temptation. "Flee youthful lusts," as St. Paul teaches Timothy. When the temptation to sin presents itself to you, leave. If a friend entices you to sin, put some real physical distance between yourself and that person.

Taylor: But that's not how temptation works. Temptation occurs in the mind. You can't pluck out your brain if it causes you to sin.

Gibbs: Temptation occurs in the mind but usually refers to something tangible which is right in front of you, which is why fleeing from temptation is possible.

Taylor: I don't understand.

Gibbs: Fleeing temptation means fleeing the things by which we are tempted. No one is tempted to gluttony in the abstract. The devil never whispers in your ear, "You should commit the sin of gluttony." Rather, we are tempted to eat that whole bag of chips or that whole pint of ice cream. You fight the temptation to eat a whole pint of ice cream by getting rid of the ice cream. Even atheists who go on diets understand that. What is true of gluttony is true of lust and theft as well.

Taylor: But overcoming temptation is about having a strong spirit.

Gibbs: Yes, a spirit which is strong enough to move our bodies away from the things which tempt us.

Taylor: But everything is a potential temptation.

Gibbs: But everything is not equally tempting to every person, which is why boys change in one locker room and girls change in another. If a man can eat a modest portion of ice cream and put the carton back into the refrigerator, fine, it is not a temptation to him. But it behooves a man to know the particular ways in which the devil goes after him. The devil is going after you through this friend. You have a friend who is blazing a trail to hell and you feel it is your duty to go with him. I am telling you to confess to your parents whatever hellish things you have done already, then tell your friend to do the same, and not go with him any further toward the flames. What I'm telling you to do is painful and embarrassing, of course, but Christ acknowledges that fighting temptation will be painful. If your right eye causes you to sin, you should pluck it out.

Taylor: You don't take the command to "pluck out your right eye" at face value and neither do I.

Gibbs: Fair enough, but I offered my interpretation. I would like to hear yours.

Taylor: When He says, "Pluck out your right eye if it causes you to sin," Christ is showing His disciples that they will never finally overcome sin, at least not in this life. The only way to truly keep yourself from sinning is to kill yourself. If a man cut off every part of his body which caused him to sin, he wouldn't have a body left. "Pluck out your right eye if it causes you to sin" is Christ's way of showing His disciples how impossibly high the standard is. This way, they will understand that all men are saved by grace, not through good works.

Gibbs: Running from Potiphar's wife worked for Joseph.

Taylor: But it is not as though Joseph never sinned again for the rest of his life.

Gibbs: If he sinned, it was not by sleeping with Potiphar's wife.

Taylor: Joseph may have triumphed in that temptation, but I am quite sure that other temptations returned.

Gibbs: Remind me again what your initial question was?

Taylor: There is a student at this school who is having a rough year. I want to know how to help him.

Gibbs: By your rationale, there is no point in helping him.

Taylor: What do you mean?

Gibbs: It seems that when we speak of you overcoming your

temptations, it was pointless to do anything because we are saved by grace, not by works, and none of us finally overcome sin in this life. When we speak of your troubled young man overcoming his temptations, you want to know what to do in order to help him.

Taylor: But I do want to help him.

Gibbs: If you help him now, who cares? He will sin again. The standard is so impossibly high—your own words—that it does not really matter if he overcomes his temptations because he is depending on the grace of God just as much as you are.

Taylor: What do I do, then?

Gibbs: Are you willing to suffer in order to help him?

Taylor: Yes.

Gibbs: Then confess whatever it is that you have hidden from your parents. Tell this troubled young man you have confessed your sins, then don't see him again until he confesses his sin to his parents as well.

Taylor: I have not really done anything worth confessing.

Gibbs: I don't believe you.

Taylor: If I told my parents what little sins I have committed because of him, they wouldn't let me see him again. Confessing these little sins to my parents would be tantamount to abandoning a friend in trouble, and I cannot do that. It is one thing to run from temptation, but it is something completely different to run from a human being in need. If someone is addicted to porn and needs to give up their phone, perhaps they should. But Jesus hung out with prostitutes, and Christians must follow His example.

Gibbs: Jesus did not hang out with prostitutes.

Taylor: Oh, my God! Have you never read those passages in the Bible? Mr. Gibbs, he absolutely did hang out with prostitutes. How do you not know this?

Gibbs: Show me.

Taylor: I don't know exactly where it is described. It is in one of the Gospels. I would have to look it up.

Gibbs: Why don't you look it up on your phone right now? I can wait.

Taylor: Fine. Here it is. While Jesus was having dinner at Matthew's house, many tax collectors and sinners came and ate with him and his disciples. When the Pharisees saw this, they asked his disciples, "Why does your teacher eat with tax collectors and sinners?" (Matthew 9:10-11)

Gibbs: For good measure, why don't you read the other passage which describes the encounter between Christ and "sinners"?

Taylor: Now the tax collectors and sinners were all gathering around to hear Jesus. But the Pharisees and the teachers of the law muttered, "This man welcomes sinners and eats with them." (Luke 15:1-2)

Gibbs: I'm not seeing where Jesus hung out with prostitutes.

Taylor: My pastor says that "sinners" is a euphemism for "prostitutes."

Gibbs: Did your pastor also tell you that the woman caught in the act of adultery was a prostitute, by any chance?

Taylor: That sounds familiar, but I am not certain I have heard that. At the same time, I am not quite sure what your argument stands to gain from bringing up that story. Christ forgave the woman caught in the act of adultery.

Gibbs: What was the last thing Christ said to that woman?

Taylor: "Go and sin no more."

Gibbs: Are you willing to say that to your troubled young man?

Taylor: Jesus could say that because He had no sin. But the Bible clearly says He hung out with prostitutes without confronting them. It doesn't say He chastised them after the meal.

Gibbs: What do you mean when you say Jesus "hung out" with them?

Taylor: He spent time with them.

Gibbs: In both the accounts you read of Christ "hanging out" with prostitutes, it was the prostitutes who came to eat with Jesus. He did not go to them. They sought Him out. What would you and your only-somewhat-compromised friends have to do in order for your troubled young man to seek you out?

Taylor: I don't know.

Gibbs: You could start by confessing your sins to your parents and telling your troubled young man to do the same. He would likely resist you, but then it would be him running from you. You would not actually have to shun him.

Taylor: What you're describing is conditional love.

Gibbs: The only way you can think to love this young man involves indulging his sin.

Taylor: Love covers a multitude of sins.

Gibbs: Hanging out with sin does not "cover" sin. You are too embarrassed of righteousness to actually cover sin. Your proposal for treating this young man's sin—or your youth pastor's proposal, rather—bolsters sin and ultimately adopts it. It astounds me how often young Christians take the claim "Jesus hung out with prostitutes" to mean, "What God really wants is for me to play Xbox and watch Netflix with my worldly friends. If I just play Xbox with them for long enough, eventually they'll become Christians."

Taylor: But if you want to share the Gospel with someone, you have to know them. You have to establish a friendship with someone and love them before they can truly hear the Gospel. If you don't show someone you love them first, the Gospel is going to come off as condemnation.

Gibbs: When St. Peter preached on Pentecost, his sermon concluded with such condemnations that the people who heard it were "cut to the heart." After the sermon, three thousand people were baptized. St. Peter did not bother establishing friendships with all three thousand of those people before he presented the Gospel to them. I hear about the importance of establishing long-term friendships with the lost before preaching the Gospel to them all the time from naïve, tender-hearted Christians who are just going off to college. They honestly believe they ought to seek out homosexuals for friends, live with them in a loving and close-knit community for several years, and then finally break it to them that God does not approve of their lifestyle.

Taylor: What's wrong with that?

Gibbs: It doesn't work. After a few years, the Christians in question no longer believe homosexuality is a sin. They come back home after college saying, "Everything changes once you actually get to know someone who is gay. Many of them are good, kind people in genuinely loving relationships, just like straight people." That's how friendship works, though. That's how influence works. As a teacher, I see it all the time. If an obedient student and a disobedient student become friends, the obedient student will become disobedient. Not the other way around. If you put a person with influenza in the same room as a healthy person, it is the influenza that rubs off, not the health.

Taylor: How are people with influenza supposed to get better?

Gibbs: By going to the doctor.

Taylor: Is a doctor not a healthy person? Does the healthy person not offer health to the sick person?

Gibbs: Yes, and how does a doctor improve the health of a sick person?

Taylor: By treating them.

Gibbs: Exactly. But so far as your troubled young man is concerned, you are not proposing anything like treatment. In order for a doctor to make a sick person well, the sick person must believe he is sick, and then he must seek the doctor out. He must submit to an examination by the doctor, which is often invasive, and then he must hear his diagnosis, even if the diagnosis is offensive. If he is willing to do all these things, he must take whatever medicine the doctor gives him, no matter how expensive. He must also undergo a regimen for improving his condition, no matter how inconvenient. That is how sick men get better. Sickness rubs off. Health does not. Your idea that good influence "rubs off" on sinners is no better than telling a man with cancer that he will get better if he takes up a job serving mashed potatoes in a hospital cafeteria.

Taylor: So, goodness is not more powerful than evil?

Gibbs: Evil does not have power. Evil is not a power, but the absence of power to do good. Of course, goodness is more powerful than evil, but this does not mean goodness is a catchier tune than evil. Wickedness is a thing we slouch into. It is easy to be wicked. Virtue, strength, and health only come by way of great effort. Being fat comes easily; being fit comes by way of sacrifice and struggle. The fit man has tamed his nature; the fat man has been tamed by his passions.

Taylor: Have you never seen a sinner change his ways, then?

Gibbs: I have seen sinners change. I have seen fools become wise, but only by Herculean effort. I have seen fools turn back, but the moment of turning back is painful and embarrassing. The Prodigal Son ultimately turns back, but only after a mortifying confrontation with his own failure. The goodness of his father does not rub off on him, but painfully breaks open within him. Neither did the righteousness of Christ rub off on the world. His righteousness came to us through His crucifixion, and if we would accept His righteousness, we must take up our own crosses, not just once, but every day.

Taylor: But I'm not a doctor. I don't know what sort of medicine to apply. That is why I came to you.

Gibbs: That is true. However, I suspect you don't really know what your troubled young man's problem is. You only see a few symptoms.

Taylor: Do you really think we ought to shun him, then? That seems so cultish.

Gibbs: Cultish? Absolutely not. You have simply accepted entirely too many fashionable ideas about "community," which is why you're having a difficult time understanding what this young man's problem is.

Taylor: What fashionable ideas? Perhaps you and I have very different beliefs on the importance of other people. "People" is one of my church's core ideals. At my church, we are taught to love people. Americans languished for too long under the idea that the lonesome cowboy was an ideal hero. At my church, we believe that people matter and that community matters. Perhaps you're just a little too content with yourself and a little too introverted.

Gibbs: Over the last twenty years, American Christians have deified the concept of "community." We cannot think of anything which is more important than furthering community, enjoying community, and fostering community. We are willing to sacrifice doctrinal purity in order to increase our communities. We are willing to patronize sin and turn a blind eye to perversion just so no one feels "cut off from the community." We believe our most fundamental duty is to other human beings, not to God, and that the most important thing we can do for other people is make them feel comfortable, needed, and loved. Consequently, we feel guilty whenever we step away from someone, no matter the reason. We have accepted the idea that whatever threatens social unity is worthless—even truth, beauty, goodness, and holiness must be sacrificed for the sake of social unity. We believe that our highest calling is to stay together; thus, anyone who claims there is something more important than staying together is a blasphemer.

Taylor: So, you do think we should shun him. You're proud of yourself for holding a minority opinion on the matter. There's a quality to cultish things that appeals to you.

Gibbs: Is it so hard to believe that a little time alone could do your troubled young man some good?

Taylor: How? I'm not his mother. My circle of friends is not his parents. It is not our place to put him in time-out.

Gibbs: "Am I my brother's keeper?"

Taylor: You know what I meant.

Gibbs: Have you never read the story of how God spoke to Elijah in "a still small voice," the kind of voice which can only be heard when one is free from distractions, noise, and other people?

Taylor: I suppose.

Gibbs: Are you familiar with all the Scriptural injunctions to keep silence? Have you never read the many proverbs which describe the need to control your tongue, say very little, and not say everything that comes into your head?

Taylor: What's the problem with not confronting and chastising my friend, then?

Gibbs: The longer we talk, the less troubled by his sin you seem to be.

Taylor: What makes you say that?

Gibbs: A lot of Christians these days take a communal, missionary approach to socially acceptable sins, but jettison that approach when it comes to unfashionable sins. For this reason, I have never heard a Christian say, "My neighbor gets drunk and beats his wife, but if I condemn him for his sin, he'll just run. I need to spend a few years getting close to him, befriending him, and taking him casseroles when he has the flu before I tell him God doesn't approve of domestic abuse." Domestic abuse is an incredibly unpopular sin at the moment, which means the same Christians who take a soft, live-in-community-before-judging approach to fashionable sins feel entirely vindicated calling the cops the first time they hear a vase hit the wall next door.

Taylor: But an actual human life is on the line.

Gibbs: They would call the cops on a neighbor who beat his dog, too.

Taylor: What's your point?

Gibbs: My point is that people who pose as missionary friends don't take their work all that seriously. I have yet to hear a Christian heading off to college say he plans on becoming friends with a bunch of racist Republicans for a few years before telling them how God feels about black people.

Taylor: Maybe that's not what racist Republicans need though.

Gibbs: So fashionable sinners need coddling and unfashionable sinners need a sermon. How convenient.

Taylor: Doesn't it say somewhere that judgment should "begin" with the house of God?

Gibbs: Great. Start with yourself.

Taylor: That's not what I meant.

Gibbs: I know. When people reference that verse, it usually means, "Let judgment begin with me confessing the sins of my fellow Christians." It also means casually implicating yourself when publicly confessing sins you don't think you've committed.

Taylor: That's plain bizarre. Who in the world casually implicates himself in the sins of others?

Gibbs: "Forgive us, Lord, for our racism" is a common prayer among those who pride themselves on not being racist at all—at least, it is a common prayer among such people when standing behind podiums, although I could not say whether they pray it often in the solitude of their own hearts. The uncomfortable truth at the center of this conversation is that helping your troubled friend will mean confessing your own sins first. There is no way around it, and when you confess what you have done, your parents will immediately ask for names. They will want to know who you were with so they can keep you from spending more time with those people, lest you do these foolish things again.

Taylor: I know. They're from an older generation that doesn't understand the importance of community. My father still prides himself on never going to the doctor.

Gibbs: How is that related?

Taylor: You must take care of yourself before you can take care of the community. Self-care is selfless.

Gibbs: Your parents have more common sense than you do, which means they are primarily concerned with what works. Better for you to go to heaven embarrassed than go to hell with your ego intact. When you confess to your father what you have done, his response will be aimed at keeping you out of court, out of the hospital, and out of the maternity ward, and that will mean cutting you off from your accomplices. I suspect, though, that not everyone in your group of seven or eight friends is equally worried about this troubled young man—at least, not equally worried for his soul.

Taylor: What are they worried about, then?

Gibbs: Like yourself, they're worried about getting caught. When you're with your friends, has anyone ever floated the idea of coming clean to your parents about everything that you've done?

Taylor: Yes.

Gibbs: Why don't you?

Taylor: For the same reason husbands don't come clean to their wives about everything they've done.

Gibbs: That's a very knowing response, although some husbands come clean to their wives about everything.

Taylor: Which husbands?

Gibbs: The husbands who came clean to their parents about everything when they were younger. If you want to be honest with your spouse when you're older, you must earn it while you're young by being honest with your parents.

Taylor: Let me be honest with you. I haven't really told you what is bothering me, which is why I haven't caved yet and admitted that I ought to tell my parents everything.

Gibbs: Fair enough.

Taylor: My pastor began this long sermon series about community last year, but I've loved my friends for a lot longer than that. I didn't need my church to tell me community is important. I understand the idea in my bones. I realized I loved my friends when I was in eighth grade—in November of my eighth-grade year. My friends mean everything to me. My friends are like my real family. I can be honest with them. I can't be honest with my parents anymore. We're too different.

Gibbs: Your parents don't love their friends the way you love your friends, do they?

Taylor: My father doesn't give a damn about his friends. He talks to his best friend on the phone once or twice a year. He has a few friends from work, but I hear about them at the dinner table. He rarely invites them over. If I were honest with my parents about my friends—about everything we've done, everything that goes on—they would tell me I couldn't see them again. They would take away my phone and I couldn't talk to them anymore. I would never see them outside of school. The thing is, because my parents don't really care that much about their friends, they would not understand what it meant to me to be cut off from my friends. They would cut me off from my friends without a second thought. They would do it as simply and easily as they told me, "No dessert for you tonight," when I was six.

Gibbs: My friends meant everything to me when I was your age as well.

Taylor: Don't pretend you're superior to me just because you outgrew your first love.

Gibbs: When I was your age, I believed my community of friends was special and that we would always be close.

Taylor: And then you married?

Gibbs: At sixteen, I did not like school, but I had perfect attendance because I was afraid of missing out on anything that happened to my friends. When I was sick, I said to myself, "But suppose something terribly important happens today and I am not around to see it? Then all my friends will have a connection to one another which I do not understand. I will be excluded," and so I told my mother I was fine and went to school.

Taylor: How long did it last?

Gibbs: Until I was twenty-seven or so.

Taylor: What happened when you were twenty-seven?

Gibbs: The same thing that happens to most people, but I am getting ahead of myself. Let me interrupt the story of my youth with a question for you. You're now seventeen. Spend a moment recalling what you were like at the age of ten. Remember the sorts of things you enjoyed in fifth grade. Remember your hobbies, the books you read, the places your parents would take you.

Taylor: I remember being ten fairly well.

Gibbs: In the last seven years, have you become more righteous? Are you more obedient now than you were in fifth grade? Have you, with every passing year, come to love your parents more? Do you pray now with greater fervor than you did seven years ago? Or, since the age of nine or ten, have you become less righteous with every passing year? Are you a little less obedient this year than you were last year? Do you think of God a little less frequently than you used to? When you survey the course of your life over the last seven years, do you see yourself inching closer and closer to God or further and further away from Him, from obedience, from honesty, from righteousness, and from prayer?

Taylor: It is the latter.

Gibbs: When do you think it is going to stop getting worse?

Taylor: Probably when I leave my family home and move off to college.

Gibbs: Is college where most young Christians turn things around?

Taylor: All I know is that I need freedom. I want to sort things out for myself. I want to choose my own church. I want to choose my own friends. I'm tired of worrying about getting caught. I want to do what I think is right. Christian adults are free to have messed-up friends. My dad has messed-up friends.

Gibbs: Does your mother not care who your father spends time with?

Taylor: No, she cares. My mother doesn't like my dad's friends.

Gibbs: Which may account for why he never sees them. Look, when I was a little child, I was like you. I was good. I was obedient. When I lied to my parents, about half the time I would go back to them a few hours later and tearfully confess the truth. When I was six, I believed my mother was very special, and that in heaven, she would have a seat very close to the throne of God Himself. I believed that she would be rewarded for her great love of her family and that everyone would acknowledge she was a remarkable human being. By the time I was fifteen, though, my parents had largely become obstacles which stood between me and the things I wanted to do. When I was a little child, I thought of my parents as the people who took me to the park, took me out for ice cream, bought me Christmas presents, told me stories, and sang and prayed with me before bed. By fifteen, I thought of my parents as the people who told me I couldn't listen to this music, couldn't watch that movie, couldn't hang out with those people. To this day, my soul still suffers from the residual effects of seeing my parents as obstacles when I was a teenager.

Taylor: If your soul hasn't recovered from the sins you committed when you were in high school, perhaps there is something seriously flawed about your soul.

Gibbs: I agree, but that flaw entered my soul when I was a teenager. It wasn't always there. The role which God intends your parents to play in your young life is so vital, so massive, so important, that the failure to love, cling to, admire, and respect your parents during your teenage years stands to skew your life, send your life on a dark, contradictory path that will only become increasingly harder to correct with every passing year.

Taylor: What role is that?

Gibbs: It's pointless to get advice from people that are your own age. That's true no matter how old you are. Your friends are as dumb as you. My friends are as dumb as me. Your friends can't see farther than you can. People your own age always tell you exactly what you want to hear. Old people never tell you what you want to hear. Have you ever noticed that?

Taylor: My youth pastor told me what I wanted to hear. He's married and has a kid, like you.

Gibbs: Is he older than twenty-seven?

ON FRIENDSHIP & FAMILY

Taylor: No, but what is your deal with twenty-seven?

Gibbs: I'll get to that, but why do you think old people never tell young people what they want to hear?

Taylor: Because they don't remember what it was like to be young. They don't understand.

Gibbs: Perhaps you think I don't understand. I'll tell you this, though. My parents regularly give me advice that I don't like, and I am forty-two years old.

Taylor: What sort of advice do they give?

Gibbs: They tell me to save my money—not a message I have ever enjoyed hearing because saving money is less fun than spending it. Older people generally tell younger people to be more frugal, more quiet, and less impulsive. The older you get, the more you stand to lose, which means you care less about excitement and more about stability. Stability allows you to retain the things you've achieved, whereas excitement puts everything you've achieved at risk. At your age, though, you have accomplished very little and so you have little to lose, which means that excitement is still very appealing. Old people know that you find excitement appealing, which is why they entrust you with very little. Nonetheless, old people raise young people. God set up the world that way.

Taylor: Then why am I so close with my friends?

Gibbs: Friends are easy to love. Family is much harder to love.

Taylor: That's not true. Love for your family comes naturally. Everyone loves their family, but not everyone has friends, which means that friends are harder to love.

Gibbs: I used to believe that, as well. It's not a sustainable belief, though. As you come to see your parents as obstacles to your happiness—as most teenagers do—you inevitably grow closer to your friends. In high school, my friends and I often spoke of friendship itself, and of the shifting loyalties of various friendships in our class and in our school. Who had a crush on who? Who was becoming more like who? My friends were very nearly a religion to me because they determined the shape of my life: where I went, what I did, what I wanted, how I consoled myself. Because my parents did not have friends the way I did, it was almost like they practiced a completely separate faith. As I passed through high school, I became increasingly distanced from my parents. This happened naturally enough. At thirteen or fourteen, I had no money and could not drive, and so I relied upon my parents for everything. By the time I was sixteen, I had a job and a car, which meant I could see my friends whenever I wanted, buy whatever music I wanted, see whatever movies struck my fancy, and so I didn't really need my parents for the things I cared about the most. What was true for me was true for all my friends as well. We all spent more and more time alone, by ourselves, away from our parents.

Taylor: Is this not simply what it means to grow up? Throughout high school, we spend less and less time with our parents, and then we graduate and move away and spend no time with them?

Gibbs: It is certainly common and the troubles it creates are common, as well.

Taylor: What sort of troubles did it create for you?

Gibbs: To this day, I don't remember if we started spending more time by ourselves and then found mischief, or if we wanted to get into mischief and so we started spending more time by ourselves. Either way, when I was sixteen, a whole bunch of my friends and I started smoking.

Taylor: Cigarettes or weed?

Gibbs: Cigarettes.

Taylor: Gross.

Gibbs: I feel the same way about TikTok. Filthy habit. I suspect that nearly every little circle of high school friends has something they keep secret from the adults. We tend to rationalize such secrets on the grounds that "the adults wouldn't understand." The thing is, it usually becomes necessary to lie in order to keep group secrets secret. For this reason, it does not really matter what the group is keeping secret—it could be cigarettes, it could be a lot less than cigarettes, but it could also be a lot more, like gossip, theft, sex, drugs, and ten thousand other things which have to do with the internet and smartphones. As soon as a group of high school friends begins lying to adults in order to keep their secrets, that group has opened itself up to the very cruel logic which goes with deception.

Taylor: And what cruel logic is that?

Gibbs: The older you get, the more you can get in exchange for a lie. When you are a little child, a lie can't get you very much. A lie might get you out of a spanking or an extra slice of cake. But when you are sixteen, the right lie might get you a lot. One of the greatest things the right lie can get you is time, time by yourself. A single lie, just a sentence or two, could get you an hour to do whatever you want. Of course, it could get you far longer than an hour. Once you are willing to lie to cover your tracks, your tracks can get bigger and dirtier.

Taylor: This all sounds so conspiratorial, though. You sound like you're talking about the mob. I really do love my parents.

Gibbs: Not as much as you love your friends—at least, not for the moment. You've entered into that long corridor of youth wherein your parents no longer make sense to you.

Taylor: How long does that last?

Gibbs: Until you're—well, you already know what the age is. Lying to your parents only makes you less inclined to spend time around them, because when you're around your parents, they like to ask questions about your life because they love you and want to know how you're doing. Depending on how many stories and secrets you are trying to keep hidden, just having a simple half-hour conversation with your parents might be rather anxiety-inducing. Over the course of my sophomore, junior, and senior years, I found myself increasingly desensitized to telling lies. While my conscience would have been troubled about lying to my parents when I was nine or ten, by seventeen or eighteen, lying to my parents was simply the price of being left alone. Lying to my parents was part of the standard operating cost of being a teenager. During my junior and senior years, the things my friends and I were keeping secret from our parents went from unsavory to illegal and dangerous. I was not part of the worst of it, but I was telling lies for my friends so they could keep various cons running. I spent the better part of high school worried that I would be found out. I came home from school nearly every day nervous that my mother would meet me at the door with a scowl and say we needed to talk.

Taylor: That sounds familiar, I confess.

Gibbs: The fact is, there was a long time wherein we were not so much friends as co-conspirators. We did not build one another up, but patiently and methodically tore one another down for several years. We started small, but, like I said, as soon as we had all agreed to lie on one another's behalf, the worst of it was fated. We enjoyed one another's company, but only because we had all agreed to be a safe haven for one another's sin. In the end, some of my friends were discovered, some of us made full confessions, and there was a massive scandal. I was eighteen at the time. To this day, sorting out our various motives would prove difficult. The fallout of our sin was unpleasant and embarrassing, and it took many years for the echo of the thing to fade.

Taylor: But it faded, right? And you all stayed together?

Gibbs: For a time. I learned a few things from the whole ordeal, but I maintained my youthful outlook on friendship. The college that most of my friends and I attended was only about a mile away from my high school, which meant my circle of friends expanded in the years which followed the scandal. At the time, I thought highly of myself due to my many friends. I thought, "My family has to love me, and I have to love them, but I have chosen to love my friends." Because I had chosen to love my friends, my soul must be more expansive than the average man. But that is all wrong. Family is far harder to love than friends are.

Taylor: But love for family comes naturally and what comes naturally comes easily. It is natural to fall asleep at night. It does not require effort. No one deserves an award for being tired at 11:00 p.m.

Gibbs: Love of family comes easily and naturally up to a certain age, but this stage of life is followed by a stage where family becomes quite difficult to love. We choose our friends, but not our family, which means that we are stuck with our families. We choose our friends based on shared interests, shared loves, and shared beliefs. Close friendship usually requires a great deal of financial and moral equality, which prevents either party from being exploited or used. Our friends rarely embarrass us with their out-of-touch opinions and unfashionable theories, but this is because we choose our friends based on their similarity to ourselves. We are less likely to hit our friends up for money than our families, which means friends are less likely to judge us than family and less likely to give us pointed advice about drinking or how quickly we spend our money. Long story short, when you are young, the fact your friends have chosen to love you makes their love seem more real than the love of your family. As you get older, though, the fact your family loves you even though they didn't choose you seems far more impressive.

Taylor: But your mother has to love you.

Gibbs: No, your mother has a duty to love you, but the love of a mother is not inevitable. Stories of mothers and fathers who murder their children are a dime a dozen nowadays. Because our society allots very few duties to young people, you do not yet understand that fulfilling a duty can be an emotionally and spiritually authentic action. Most of the duties you fulfill are for school and you do not like school, which means you think of duty as a kind of banal, bureaucratic necessity which inexplicably pacifies the people in charge. On the other hand, responsible adults understand that people who fulfill their duties make life possible—not only for the people they love but for all the irresponsible people out there who shirk their duties.

Taylor: You still haven't told me what happens at the age of twenty-seven.

Gibbs: At twenty-seven, you rediscover your parents. They begin to make sense to you once again. By twenty-seven, you've lost touch with most of your friends from high school and college.

Taylor: The fact you lost touch with friends from your youth doesn't mean everybody does.

Gibbs: True. However, unless all your friends from high school go to the same college, then all your friends from college get jobs in the same town, you will lose touch with one another.

Taylor: You graduated twenty years ago, though. That was well before the age of social media.

Gibbs: It wasn't before the age of telephones and the postal service, though. There have always been ways of keeping in touch.

Taylor: Then why didn't you keep in touch?

Gibbs: When you move to a new place, you form new friendships. Those friendships are born out of shared struggles and shared accomplishments. The friends who are physically near you are the people you eat with, celebrate with, go to church with. They are the people who give you a ride when your car is in the shop, the people who bring you dinner when you are sick, the people you gossip with, sin with, repent with. You can keep in touch with friends who are far away, but it is very difficult to share your life with such people. "Keeping in touch" is not the same thing as friendship. It often means hearing about all the things our old friends have done lately with their new friends.

Taylor: That's depressing.

Gibbs: A little, yes. There may be a few rare friendships—perhaps just one or two in your whole life—which survive great distance, but not many. Of course, most people move away for college and then move away four years after that when they find work. There are only so many hours of the day. If you resolve to remain close with your high school friends after everyone goes their separate ways, it will mean you have very little to offer the people you work with, go to church with, and live with. By the time you're really getting somewhere in your career, you're married. You are tired of moving. You no longer want excitement. You want stability. You recognize in yourself the same frustrations you recall from your youth. You begin to understand your parents.

Taylor: And nearly everyone stays in touch with their parents.

Gibbs: We also feel a duty to visit our parents, and they feel a duty to visit us. We do not feel the same duties toward our friends. We visit our friends when it is convenient and because it is pleasant. Your relationship with your family will never go away. Once a daughter, always a daughter. Once a brother, always a brother. The same cannot be said for friendship, which begins to fade when it is not fed. You have a reason to think of your brother whenever you hear the word "brother." A thousand things within nature remind us of our mothers and fathers on a daily basis. Again, the same cannot be said for friends we have not seen in years.

Taylor: I understand. But you say all of this as though it couldn't happen any other way. It almost seems as though I have to become distant from my parents, they have to get in the way, I have to leave my friends, and I have to rediscover my parents ten years from now. Or are you telling me all this so I don't make the same mistakes you did?

Gibbs: I wouldn't say everyone is fated to lose touch with their parents during adolescence or that everyone is fated to rediscover them later, but this conversation began about a troubled young man whom you want to help. You are afraid to help him, though, because you believe you will lose touch with your friends if you do. There's a kind of synergy to your friendship because you all have a few things to keep secret, but the secrets you have now are nothing compared with the secrets you'll make in college, which means I don't think your high school friendship is all that stable to begin with. Confessing your sin now and being cut off from your friends for a little while might actually give you stable ground upon which to build a real friendship later.

Taylor: I can't really be friends with my parents now, though. We just don't have that kind of relationship.

Gibbs: That's okay. You don't need your parents to be your friends now. You need them to be parents. Friends are not authorities and authorities are not friends. Not every good and meaningful relationship has to boil down to friendship.

Taylor: What if I want my mother to be my friend?

Gibbs: When your relationship is not entirely built around duty, obedience, and obligation, that might be possible. Your relationship with your parents is far more durable than your relationship with your friends, which means that all the time and effort you put into your relationship with your mother will come back to you and to your children someday.

Taylor: If I'm going to rediscover my parents at twenty-seven, does it really matter what happens to our relationship now?

Gibbs: Not every teenager who decides his parents are obstacles in high school rediscovers them twelve years later. Bad friendships simply dissolve, but it is possible to have a bad relationship with your parents for your entire life. I have never heard an adult say, "I have had a bad relationship with my friend Bill since we were freshmen." In other words, you're stuck with your parents for the next forty years. You might as well make that relationship a good one.

Taylor: Then what are high school friendships worth?

Gibbs: The fact that most high school friendships do not last does not mean they are worthless. Very few earthly things last forever. Besides, there is something very beautiful about the intensity of feeling, the verve, and the liveliness which is shared between young friends. Twenty years from now, you may not even remember the names of all your old friends, but you can still serve them today. You can still love them, do good for them, and help them now.

DIALOGUE 3

On Video Games

Toby: What do you think of video games?

Gibbs: Oh, playing a round or two of *Tetris* every few months is probably not going to kill anyone.

Toby: That is not what I meant.

Gibbs: I know.

Toby: I wanted to know what you thought about video games as a hobby.

Gibbs: You mean the kind of thing which a fellow spends a few hours doing every day? The kind of thing which he talks about and thinks about at length?

Toby: Yes.

Gibbs: You really don't need to ask my opinion about video games, do you? I teach old books. You know what I think about video games.

Toby: I want to hear you say it, though. I don't think video games are that bad.

Gibbs: Why not?

Toby: Did you play video games when you were young?

Gibbs: Off and on. I had a Nintendo for a year or two when I was a little kid, but my parents became convinced that using it gave me a short temper. I played computer games off and on when I was in middle school. When I was in high school, I spent a year putting quarters into a *Mortal Kombat 3* arcade game at the mall. So, yes, I played video games when I was young, but not really the way a lot of kids play video games today.

Toby: What was *Mortal Kombat* like when you were in high school?

Gibbs: Same as today. Ripping people's heads off, mutilating their corpses, that sort of thing.

Toby: Not all games are like that, though.

Gibbs: What is your point?

Toby: Today, most video games have nuanced and detailed stories. These games can be violent, but there is a lot more to them than violence. The characters are amazing. They have complex backstories and motivations and desires. Some games are almost like novels.

Gibbs: Do gamers tend to read a lot of novels, as well?

Toby: Not really.

Gibbs: If gamers enjoy nuanced and detailed stories so much, why don't they read more novels?

Toby: Well, a video game is like a novel, but it is a lot more fun than a novel.

Gibbs: Would you say it is easier for a young man to get into video games than novels?

Toby: Of course.

Gibbs: The fact that video games are both easier and more fun than novels means the two are really nothing alike, which is why gamers don't read many novels.

Toby: But stories are good. In theology class, we hear about the importance of story all the time.

Gibbs: What is "the importance of story"?

Toby: Just the importance of hearing stories. Stories can show you how to be a better person and how to feel compassion for other people.

Gibbs: What stories? Any stories or only certain stories?

Toby: Good stories.

Gibbs: So good stories are good for people. That isn't exactly rocket science.

Toby: People need stories, though.

Gibbs: That is a very popular claim over the last ten years or so. Stories have always been with us and always will be, though, so I don't understand why Christians have lately come to think the claim that stories are important is so profound.

Toby: Video games might be different from novels, but they can also tell good stories. When you were a kid, pretty much every video game involved saving a princess. Now, there are games where a guy's wife dies, and he must figure out how to cope with it. That's the whole game.

Gibbs: How much time have you spent playing this game?

Toby: I tried it once. Games like that are common.

Gibbs: Why did you only try it once?

Toby: It was a bit dull.

Gibbs: But the story was good?

Toby: Yes. The story was quite deep, and many people got into it.

Gibbs: If the story was deep, why didn't you keep playing the game?

Toby: It just wasn't my thing.

Gibbs: Deep stories aren't your thing?

Toby: Not all deep stories.

Gibbs: That is why I don't think highly of video games. Gamers often defend video games on the grounds they have deep stories, but given that gamers don't read much, I don't buy that defense. If gamers were graduating into higher and better stories, and if video games were a common gateway into Russian literature, that would be another matter. The fact is that gamers don't really like stories unless those stories are attached to games.

Toby: Why is that so bad?

Gibbs: A game is fundamentally different than a book or a film.

Toby: How so?

Gibbs: A game exists for the amusement of the players. What is the chief reason why people quit playing a game?

Toby: It's no fun. Little kids quit playing Monopoly when they know they are going to lose.

Gibbs: Agreed. The point of a game is to have fun, which is why adults often take a handicap when playing chess against their children. It's no fun if you win in six moves. The challenge is what makes it fun. The better the game, the more fun it is to play.

Toby: So, what's the problem with that?

Gibbs: I simply don't think having fun is very important. People will continue to read a novel which isn't any fun, though, because they know the novel is good for them. We read classics because they are good for us. I have often heard it said, "I wish I liked *Paradise Lost*, but I don't," or, "I wish I enjoyed Wagner's operas, but I never developed a taste for that kind of music." I have never heard someone say, "I wish I enjoyed *Halo*, but I don't." That is because video games exist to please us. If they do not please us, they are worthless to us. Sometimes a novel is fun, but very good novels are usually hard work. We keep reading difficult novels because we want something more than mere fun.

Toby: But there are some video games that are really hard which people play anyway.

Gibbs: Why?

Toby: Because even though the games are hard, they're fun.

Gibbs: It always comes back to fun. If a fellow only plays a few rounds of *Tetris* every once in a while, he has not blown fun out of proportion. Fun occupies an appropriate place in his life. However, to spend hours every day in the pursuit of fun is simply very shallow.

ON VIDEO GAMES

Toby: But video games are not just about having fun. They're also about problem-solving.

Gibbs: Were human beings not very good at solving problems before video games?

Toby: I don't know. But recent studies have shown that playing video games actually makes you smarter.

Gibbs: What studies?

Toby: Studies that scientists conducted which involve brain imaging. I read about it on *Lifehacker*.

Gibbs: I'll hazard the guess that you didn't read the actual studies which were published.

Toby: So?

Gibbs: I will also hazard the guess that you would not understand the studies if you tried to read them.

Toby: So?

Gibbs: So, studies which you did not read—and which you could not understand, even if you tried—told you that doing something fun is making you smarter?

Toby: Yes.

Gibbs: I'll have you note that you were the first person in this argument to say, "Recent studies show…" I generally quit listening to anyone whose argument depends on "Recent studies show…" because it means their position is not really supported by philosophy or theology. Nonetheless, I have to ask: have you heard about recent studies which suggest the effects of video games on the brain are similar to the effects of pornography?

Toby: No.

Gibbs: I have not read these studies, though the conclusions they draw come as no surprise to someone who has been studying and lecturing on sensuality, temptation, and virtue for over a decade.

Toby: Why?

Gibbs: From time to time, I hear students argue that video games help with problem-solving or critical thinking, which sounds vaguely scientific. Back in the early '90s, my friends and I told adults that video games "improved hand-eye coordination." We didn't have any idea what it meant, but it also sounded scientific. Americans are never ones to pass up some vaguely scientific claim which supports their desire to do something they already like to do. There will always be some huckster out there telling you that "such and such is actually good for you." At the end of the day, though, video games are the opposite of delayed gratification. Video games are fun right now, which is why people become addicted to them. People do not usually get addicted to things which will be profitable later. Rather, people pry themselves away from things that are fun now to do a few things which will be profitable later, then run back to amusing themselves as quickly as possible.

Toby: But some people get paid to play video games professionally.

Gibbs: Your point?

Toby: Playing video games can be beneficial. You cannot really argue that something is a complete waste of time when some people are getting paid to do it.

Gibbs: Would you say that prostitution is a waste of time?

Toby: Prostitution is wrong.

Gibbs: Agreed. But is it a waste of time?

Toby: You see my point, though, don't you? Basketball players get paid to play a game, but you claimed games are merely for fun. Video games are just a new kind of sport, though. Video games will be thought of just like basketball or baseball or football in fifty years.

Gibbs: Perhaps. The average NBA career is less than five years long, though. The average NFL career lasts less than four years. Most pro athletes quit playing sports before they are thirty. How long is the average pro-gamer career?

Toby: I don't know.

Gibbs: As a teacher, I'm typically unimpressed when dollar figures are attached to various kinds of work. A line of work ought to be dignified in itself, not justifiable purely on monetary grounds. That said, I find the dollar figures attached to professional gaming particularly unimpressive. The "salaries" which pro gamers earn are little more than advertisements for the games they play. Assuming a career in pro gaming lasts twice as long as an NBA career, what would you say a gamer is prepared to do by the time he is forced to quit gaming at the age of 27 or 28?

Toby: What do NBA players do after they retire?

Gibbs: Become truck drivers. Open restaurants. Work for UPS. Around two-thirds of all NBA players and NFL players go broke within a few years after they retire.

Toby: A gamer could become a truck driver.

Gibbs: Would someone who played video games for ten years be willing to drive a truck for a living?

Toby: Sure.

Gibbs: Why?

Toby: Why would a gamer be any less willing to drive a truck or open a restaurant than a basketball player?

Gibbs: As a teacher, I find gamers pretty easy to spot.

Toby: How so?

Gibbs: Before I answer that question, what do you think I'm going to say? What are the qualities of a gamer which make a gamer identifiable to a teacher?

Toby: Well, I bet they're probably good at problem-solving.

Gibbs: What kind of problems?

Toby: I don't know. Puzzles.

Gibbs: Can you give me an example of a literature puzzle?

Toby: Maybe not literature, but other classes have puzzles.

Gibbs: Theology puzzles?

Toby: Maybe it's more of a math thing.

Gibbs: Are there math puzzles?

Toby: There are math problems.

Gibbs: So, gamers are good at math?

Toby: Yes.

Gibbs: Even though games have rich stories, like novels, gamers are especially good at math?

Toby: Yes.

Gibbs: Why?

Toby: Because games involve solving puzzles.

Gibbs: Do novels involve solving puzzles, as well?

Toby: Not really.

Gibbs: What about *Jane Eyre*? It seems like there are a lot of puzzles in that novel.

Toby: I haven't read it.

Gibbs: What novels have you read?

Toby: I'm not into novels.

Gibbs: Why not?

Toby: They're kind of boring.

Gibbs: What kind of puzzles are video game players good at solving?

Toby: Well, a lot of games involve finding things which are hidden. Some games involve figuring out ways around walls, over walls, and other obstacles.

Gibbs: So, in a video game, when your avatar comes to a wall and can't get over it, what do you do?

Toby: You could look for a bomb that would blow up the wall, or you could look for a magic potion that would create a door through the wall.

Gibbs: And you're claiming this is an instance of... what exactly?

Toby: Problem-solving.

Gibbs: So, if you personally came to a wall which you couldn't get over, you would begin looking for a magic potion?

Toby: No.

Gibbs: What would you do?

Toby: I don't know. Look for a ladder.

Gibbs: And what do you imagine someone who had never played video games would do in the same circumstance?

Toby: I don't know.

Gibbs: Might they look for a ladder?

Toby: Maybe.

Gibbs: What if there was no ladder?

Toby: I don't know.

Gibbs: Does using a ladder to get over a wall not seem like an obvious solution to you?

Toby: I guess so.

Gibbs: It doesn't seem to me like problem-solving is a unique talent of those who play video games. Could you suggest another way in which gamers could be easily identified by their teachers?

Toby: I don't know. I just think they are probably good problem solvers.

Gibbs: Could you give an example of a real-world problem which video gamers are uniquely suited to solving?

Toby: It's really more of a way of thinking than a knack for anything in particular.

Gibbs: A way of thinking about what?

Toby: Puzzles and games.

Gibbs: Could you give me an example of a puzzle from a video game which seems analogous to a real-world problem?

Toby: Like I said, it's more of a way that gamers think, not something in particular that they think about.

Gibbs: How about I give you an example of a real-world problem and you use a video game to tell me how to solve it?

ON VIDEO GAMES

Toby: Okay.

Gibbs: Your wife is possessed by a demon.

Toby: Mr. Gibbs, come on. That's not a real-world problem.

Gibbs: Fine. You're right. Your wife thinks she is possessed by a demon.

Toby: Nobody thinks they are possessed by a demon anymore.

Gibbs: Are there not video games where characters become possessed by demons?

Toby: There are.

Gibbs: Do those games not teach problem-solving lessons about dealing with actual demonic possession?

Toby: No.

Gibbs: Here's a real-world problem: you eat too much and so you are fat, but you only wish you cared enough to do something about it. Any video games which can help with that?

Toby: Those are complicated problems.

Gibbs: These are exactly the kind of problems which novels deal with, though. Novels deal with temptation, vanity, depression, sadness, melancholy, fear, pride, lust, earthly-mindedness, envy, and self-deception. Novels deal with complex subjects, like people who become addicted to sensual pleasures. Novels describe how sensuality wrecks the soul. Novels deal with interpersonal problems which arise between people who simultaneously love one another and hate one another. Novels treat the human ego as a labyrinth which can be escaped. Novels deal with hidden hatreds and the mystical means by which self-renunciation can convert bitterness into hope. Your claim that video games help people solve puzzles by teaching them to look for magic potions is simply laughable. When teachers need to identify gamers, they don't look for problem solvers. They look for tired students who are easily bored, say very little, and talk about video games a lot outside of class.

Toby: What do people who read a lot of novels talk about outside of class?

Gibbs: The world. Everything and everyone in the world. Why the world is the way it is.

Toby: Doesn't that seem a bit generous?

Gibbs: What kind of video games do you play? Do you play the kind of games where you pretend to murder other people?

Toby: I mean—

Gibbs: Any reason I should believe you don't have a warped sense of what generosity is?

Toby: That's kind of harsh.

Gibbs: If you want to play video games, just do it and feel guilty about it. Don't try to justify it, though. You are far better off playing games and wishing you didn't than you are inventing specious reasons why games are good for you. If you first admit to yourself (and to God) that you feel guilty about wasting so many hours of your life, then you can repent of your foolishness, and eventually, God can go to work on you.

Toby: That's definitely harsh.

Gibbs: People who commit too much time to having fun usually complain that the world is a harsh place. We're going to get over this, though. I'm going to help you. Here, borrow my copy of *Jane Eyre*, and we can talk next week about the kind of problems you're going to spend the rest of your life solving.

DIALOGUE 4

On Disagreeing with Your Church

Lucas: Mr. Gibbs, we got into this long discussion about infant baptism in theology class and heard about all these different beliefs regarding baptism. What do you think? Should we baptize infants?

Gibbs: Should who baptize babies? You?

Lucas: No. Should anyone baptize babies? What is your personal belief on the matter?

Gibbs: That is not a matter about which I have a personal belief. I do what my church tells me to do.

Lucas: And what does your church tell you to do?

Gibbs: My church baptizes babies.

Lucas: Then why didn't you just say so?

Gibbs: Because you asked, "Should we baptize infants?" and it matters an awful lot who is being asked the question. Are babies baptized at your church?

Lucas: No.

Gibbs: Then you should not baptize babies. You should obey those whom God has placed in authority over you.

Lucas: That seems so relativistic.

Gibbs: Why?

Lucas: Do you obey your church willingly or unwillingly?

Gibbs: People do things begrudgingly, but never unwillingly. "If the will won't will, nothing can force it," as Dante teaches.

Lucas: Do you wish your church didn't baptize babies?

Gibbs: No, I am happy they do.

Lucas: Then it is your personal belief that babies should be baptized, and you are telling me to do something which you believe wrong.

Gibbs: This might seem terribly nit-picky, but I am not sure you and I mean the same thing when we refer to "personal beliefs." It is my personal belief that Sofia Coppola is a great filmmaker. It is my personal belief that video games are a waste of time. However, it is not my personal belief that babies should be baptized. I personally participate in the corporate faith of my church that babies should be baptized, but my belief that babies should be baptized was not arrived at "personally."

Lucas: So, it would be wrong for me to baptize a baby?

Gibbs: Under some circumstances, sure. But the same goes for me.

Lucas: Like what?

Gibbs: If you brought a bucket of water to a shopping mall and walked around baptizing the babies of strangers.

Lucas: Well, that would obviously be wrong.

Gibbs: Why?

Lucas: No one has the right to do that.

Gibbs: Agreed. Why else?

Lucas: I've never heard of anyone doing that.

Gibbs: Yes, that is generally a good reason to avoid doing something. Why else?

Lucas: It is just plain weird.

Gibbs: Yes, it would be immoderate and imprudent. What is more, your church would not condone such a thing. And while it does not really matter for this conversation, neither would my church condone you doing such a thing. So, we agree that babies should only be baptized under certain circumstances.

Lucas: But the "circumstances" at your church are different than the "circumstances" at my church, right?

Gibbs: Yes.

Lucas: So, your church thinks my church is wrong, and you think my church is wrong.

Gibbs: Where do you go to church?

Lucas: First Baptist.

Gibbs: The matter is not that I think your church is wrong, but that I have sworn obedience and loyalty to my church instead. I know very little about your church. You should be loyal and obedient to your church though.

Lucas: Even if they teach wrong things?

Gibbs: How much do you actually know about your church?

Lucas: What do you mean?

Gibbs: How old is your denomination?

Lucas: I'm not sure.

ON DISAGREEING WITH YOUR CHURCH

Gibbs: Does your church have a statement of faith?

Lucas: I think so.

Gibbs: What does it say?

Lucas: I have not read it.

Gibbs: How is your church different than a Lutheran church or a Methodist church?

Lucas: Again, I don't know.

Gibbs: Who are the most important theologians in the last hundred years of your denomination's history?

Lucas: Look, all I know is that my church does not baptize babies, but I believe they should. I have heard the arguments on both sides and, like yourself, I think the arguments in favor of infant baptism are stronger.

Gibbs: You don't sound like you're in much of a position to judge your church.

Lucas: Why not?

Gibbs: By your own admission, you simply do not know very much about your church. You are unfamiliar with the doctrines of your church and the history of your church. You have conducted a very brief study of one particular doctrinal matter and now believe yourself in a position to go shopping for doctrines you find more attractive. It is very dangerous to treat all the churches and all the doctrines of the world like products on a shelf that can be purchased or passed over as they suit you. Treating religion like a product only makes people shallow and arrogant.

Lucas: But you have also admitted that you do not understand every doctrine your church teaches, and yet you believe those doctrines anyway. It is not as though someone needs a PhD from Duke Divinity School just to know what is true about God.

Gibbs: Of course. Off the top of my head, I don't know what my church teaches about, say, the book of Enoch, but I accept the teaching, whatever it is. In the same way I do not know what a mitochondrion does, I will gladly accept whatever a science textbook claims about the matter. But such a model of belief is entirely different than what you are proposing.

Lucas: How so?

Gibbs: I'm obedient to the science textbook's claims about the mitochondria, and I am obedient to what my church teaches about the book of Enoch. You might enjoy the fact that another church baptizes babies, but you're not being obedient to that church.

Lucas: Are you saying I should be obedient to my church?

Gibbs: At the ripe old age of sixteen? Absolutely. At sixteen, being obedient to your church matters far more to God than a rogue search for theological truth, especially given the fact that your search

ON DISAGREEING WITH YOUR CHURCH

is being conducted with such cheap tools. If you have not bothered to read your own church's statement of faith, I simply don't believe theology matters all that much to you.

Lucas: Fine, but this one particular issue matters to me.

Gibbs: Good. Let us see how much it matters to you over the next twelve months. Talk with your pastor about it. Talk with the elders at your church about it.

Lucas: I really got you wrong. I thought you would be pleased that someone believed something that your church taught.

Gibbs: If that belief is not the result of obedience and loyalty, then it matters very little. I could tell you about a hundred other doctrines my church teaches, and you might be sympathetic to a dozen or so, but it would not matter to me any more than it would matter to the Chinese government that you enjoyed Tan Dun's score to *Crouching Tiger, Hidden Dragon*.

Lucas: Don't you want me to be obedient to the Truth?

Gibbs: The Truth is a thing which has been painstakingly revealed to men by men, by God, by nature, and by the mystical institution of the Church through the crucible of time. The Truth is not a thing which a rudderless novice suddenly sets out to find on his own.

Lucas: Are you saying I should believe everything my church teaches?

Gibbs: I'm saying you should be obedient to the government of your church.

Lucas: What if my pastor started teaching there were four persons in the Trinity? What if my pastor preaches a sermon telling everyone in the congregation to commit suicide?

Gibbs: Whenever the subject of obedience to anyone or anything comes up, modern people always ask that sort of question.

Lucas: What sort of question did I just ask?

Gibbs: A hypothetical question involving some improbable, outlandish scenario.

Lucas: Don't you think a Christian should have a plan for what to do if his church began teaching heresy?

Gibbs: Are you aware that for thousands of years, sane and productive human beings had long conversations about loyalty and obedience without ever lapsing into bizarre hypothetical scenarios like the ones I just mentioned? Modern Americans, even American Christians, cannot talk about loyalty for more than two seconds without hedging their bets. We care more about imagining strange, unlikely scenarios in which we would get to rebel than we do about training our hearts to obedience in day-to-day matters. We think it is reasonable to maintain an ongoing posture of skepticism toward everything our churches do and say simply because we can imagine our churches telling us to do awful things. You are no better than a man who has a dream one night that his wife stabs him and, upon waking, never trusts her with more than a butter knife for the rest of their marriage. At the end of the day, it is far more likely that you will begin believing there are four persons in the Trinity than it is your church will begin teaching there are four persons in the Trinity.

Lucas: But what about all the cults out there that con people into doing evil things? Wouldn't it be better if the people in those cults had thought like individuals?

Gibbs: And what about all those individuals out there who con themselves into doing evil things? Would those individuals not be better off if they acted according to the dictates and precepts of some longstanding institution?

Lucas: What would you say to someone who was in a cult? Would you tell them to be loyal and obedient to their cult leader?

Gibbs: Of course not. I would probably tell such a person to go back to whatever they were doing before joining the cult. Cults tend to be short-lived, though, which means they don't last long enough to become traditions, and I have little confidence in new things, especially when it comes to religious matters. You are comparing your little Baptist church to a cult, though.

Lucas: This all sounds really suspicious. What you are saying boils down to, "Shut up and fall in line." Truth, beauty, and goodness take a back seat to doing as you are told.

Gibbs: That is somewhat true. As a teacher of classic literature, I pursue truth, beauty, and goodness, but I do not believe I am free to define these things as I like or pursue them however I choose. Along with St. Augustine, Boethius, Aquinas, and so forth, I believe truth, beauty, and goodness are the proper objects of human longing, but knowledge of these things did not simply fall from the sky. As I said, it has been slowly and patiently revealed over thousands of years by human beings and human institutions; I must pursue these things in a proper and orderly way lest I hurt myself.

Lucas: How could the pursuit of truth possibly hurt someone?

Gibbs: I would not let a child pursue truth in the middle of a busy intersection.

Lucas: Fine, but you have to admit that I have found the truth. Perhaps I found it in the middle of a busy intersection, but I managed to get back to the sidewalk holding the truth, and I'm not simply going to throw it away. I believe what you believe, at least so far as infant baptism goes, and I doubt you're going to argue me back to the beliefs of my Baptist church. I can't un-ring the bell of truth I have heard. That is not how belief works, right? "If the will won't will, nothing can force it," like you said. I cannot simply snap my fingers and return to my old beliefs about baptism.

Gibbs: That is all true. But what you do with your newfound beliefs about baptism is a matter over which you have some control.

Lucas: What should I do with my beliefs?

Gibbs: Do what Mary did. Treasure them up in your heart. Study. Contemplate. Wait. Be submissive to your parents and to your elders, just as Christ was "obedient" (Luke 2:51) to Mary and Joseph when He was young. Do not style yourself as a reformer and begin persuading all your friends from youth group of your new belief. The one exception you hold to the teachings of your church can be used as leverage to dismiss whatever your pastor tells you to do. After all, the fact that your pastor is wrong about one thing might mean he is wrong about any matter which rubs you the wrong way.

Lucas: But I cannot in good conscience go on repeating doctrinal claims I believe to be false.

Gibbs: Which is why I have encouraged you to be quiet. How long have you been persuaded that baptizing infants is right?

Lucas: For several weeks now.

Gibbs: If you can hold to the belief for the next several years, I will be impressed. At sixteen, though, you have just come into your own. You have lately begun moving out of the stage of life wherein, "Because that's what my parents believe," is a viable thing to say. You must take responsibility for your thoughts and beliefs. Of course, as soon as you take responsibility for your beliefs, you also realize it is possible to believe differently from your parents. At the age of ten or eleven, that's not really possible. By sophomore year of high school, it is possible to argue with your parents, and there is a thrill in claiming to believe something other than what your church teaches. It makes you feel very independent, very grown up.

Lucas: What do you mean by "claiming to believe something other than what your church teaches"? Do you doubt the authenticity of my belief in infant baptism?
Gibbs: Yes. At your age, claiming to believe something other than what your parents or church teaches is a pain for them, but not for

you. You get to pretend to be brave and claim that you "have to hold firmly to your convictions," while everyone else has to figure out how to keep you from becoming a self-righteous embarrassment to the family. I will accept the authenticity of your rogue new belief only when you have to take responsibility for it, which is to say when you are willing to suffer for it, which is another reason why I commend keeping your mouth shut for the next few years.

Lucas: I don't understand.

Gibbs: If you want to tell the pastor or elders of your church about your new belief, fine. They should hear you argue your point. But the pain which will come from not mentioning your special new belief to your classmates and friends from church—the suffering which besets the modern man's heart when he has a reason to believe himself special and yet he cannot disclose that secret to his peers—well, that pain and suffering over the next two years will either prove untenable and you will simply forget your brave new belief, or the pain will refine the belief of all its selfishness and arrogance so you are free to pursue it with simplicity of heart once you are out on your own.

Lucas: So, it might be better for me to forget all about my search for the truth?

Gibbs: I am not convinced that you are actually searching for the truth. If you are willing to go doctrinally rogue at the age of sixteen, God knows what you would be willing to do at the age of twenty-six.
Lucas: What do you mean?

ON DISAGREEING WITH YOUR CHURCH

Gibbs: Right now, you have strayed from your church's teaching on baptism. Granted, the belief you have strayed into is a viable position, but I can't tell yet whether it is the truth of the new position which you find attractive or whether the attraction is that the position is forbidden by those in authority over you. If it is the latter, which I think likely, you won't hold the position for very long. If you started attending a church which held to infant baptism, you could easily stray from that position into something even more novel and daring, like baptizing animals or baptizing the dead. Christianity just isn't a religion for people looking for excitement.

DIALOGUE 5

On Good Taste

Sam: At what age do you think a Christian can handle watching an R-rated movie?

Gibbs: What does it mean to "handle" an R-rated movie?

Sam: To not be affected by it.

Gibbs: Why would anyone want to watch a movie that had no effect? How dull.

Sam: I mean a film that had no negative effect.

Gibbs: Are we going to pretend that all R-rated movies are basically the same?

Sam: No, I suppose not. Over the weekend, I watched *The Wolf of Wall Street*, and when I told some other students about it over lunch, they said it was wrong to watch it.

Gibbs: When you speak of R-rated movies you certainly don't mess around. You proceed directly to a film so lurid it even made unbaptized media outlets blush. And how did you respond to your classmates? Did you tell them it was, in fact, good and virtuous to watch *The Wolf of Wall Street*?

Sam: Not quite, but I argued that as long as the viewer was spiritually prepared to handle such a film, it was not wrong to watch it.

Gibbs: Jesus Christ fasted and prayed in the wilderness for forty days to spiritually prepare for His temptation. How did you prepare to watch *The Wolf of Wall Street*?

Sam: I would say I have been preparing for years, actually. I was raised in a Bible-believing household and so I know how to rightly divide truth from falsehood. I have a resolutely Christian worldview, which enables me to critique arts and culture with objective standards. Besides this, I know quite a bit about filmmaking, so I am able to appreciate Scorsese's skill in storytelling. When I watch an R-rated film, I am able to "plunder the Egyptians," as they say. I can harvest and retain the good things a film offers and strain out anything that might be damaging.

Gibbs: I see. What would it look like if you could not "handle" such a film?

Sam: If I knew I could not handle a certain film, I would not watch it.

ON GOOD TASTE

Gibbs: That is not what I meant. If two young men watch *The Wolf of Wall Street* and one can handle it and the other could not handle it, how would that difference be manifested?

Sam: I think the fellow who could not handle the film would be tempted to the sorts of bad behavior depicted in it. Or he might fall prey to the deceitful and vain philosophies of men.

Gibbs: How exactly do you "sort" that kind of content out?

Sam: By identifying false claims and condemning them. A Biblical worldview is a sort of filter that prevents the destructive and false things in a movie from taking root in my soul.

Gibbs: Do you also have a filter that keeps images of nude women from entering your eyes? A filter that keeps vulgarity and obscenity from entering your ears?

Sam: It is one thing to see and hear those things, but another thing to be damaged or changed by them, which I am not. In the same way a healthy body can filter out toxins, a healthy soul can filter out toxic ideas.

Gibbs: An image of a nude woman is not merely an idea, though, which is part of the appeal.

Sam: Can we not get entirely hung up on the matter of a nipple or two? We both know that a great film stands or falls on something more.

Gibbs: I will leave that particular objection for the time being. Your claim that the body and mind are alike proves far too much, though. While I agree that the body is capable of filtering out certain toxins, you seem to think that merely identifying the hazardous content in a thing somehow makes that thing safe, which is absurd. Whether or not a man knows there is gin in a martini, drinking four will get him drunk. Likewise, if a man is allergic to shellfish, merely saying the words "I am allergic to these things" before downing an oyster will not keep him from breaking out in hives. If a man eats half a birthday cake for dessert every night, a knowledge of how many calories he is ingesting will not keep him from getting fat.

Sam: But knowledge of a danger is capable of neutralizing the danger. We tell our friends, "Watch out for the last step on the back patio," so they don't trip. We put signs in front of bridges which say "Slippery When Wet" so people know to slow down.

Gibbs: A "Slippery When Wet" sign implies drivers ought to do something, though. They must slow down. They must change their behavior. What you are suggesting is that merely knowing a certain bridge is slippery means a driver doesn't need to slow down.

Sam: What makes you say that?

Gibbs: Because knowledge that a certain film is filthy and lurid does not alter your behavior. You watch it anyway. A man with a little common sense acts according to what he knows, but you seem to think knowledge excuses a man from acting. If a man knows there is liquor in the punch, he does not drink four tumblers full before driving home. If a man with a shellfish allergy hears there are mussels in the bouillabaisse, he does not eat it.

Sam: Are there films which you enjoy, but which you would not let your young daughters watch?

Gibbs: Of course.

Sam: Why is that?

Gibbs: Because those films deal with subjects they are too young to understand without being spiritually harmed by them.

Sam: But you are old enough to deal with those subjects in a responsible way?

Gibbs: Yes.

Sam: So there is a certain amount of maturity, wisdom, and experience that make a man capable of dealing with dicey subjects— while those with less maturity and wisdom are not yet ready?

Gibbs: No matter how wise a man is, if he has a shellfish allergy, he cannot eat mussels.

Sam: He can if he outgrows his shellfish allergy.

Gibbs: And so seeking out lurid movies is a sign of growth? A sign of maturity?

Sam: Being able to handle such movies is.

Gibbs: If you are capable of finding redeeming features in *The Wolf of Wall Street* at the age of seventeen, I suppose you'll be capable of writing a dissertation for Princeton Theological Seminary about *Debbie Does Dallas* by the time you're twenty-four.

Sam: Ah, the old slippery slope argument.

Gibbs: If I could find redeeming qualities to *Debbie Does Dallas*, why not watch it? How many redeeming qualities would I need to find to make such a film worth my time?

Sam: By the time I write my dissertation, I will be capable of interpreting the films I have already seen on a deeper level.

Gibbs: You think you will be revisiting *The Wolf of Wall Street* for years to come, then?

Sam: Of course. I plan to keep studying and writing about film in college.

Gibbs: You write about film now?

Sam: Yes.

Gibbs: I didn't know that.

Sam: I thought everyone knew. That does sort of change things. If you didn't know I wrote about film, some of your objections make sense. You see, I believe that talking through a film is a big part of processing it, handling it, working out the theological and philosophical problems with it. I wouldn't advise anyone to watch *The Wolf of Wall Street* and then go straight to bed.

Gibbs: Why not?

Sam: For the same reason a fellow who eats a big slab of cake every night had better spend a good bit of time at the gym, as well.

Gibbs: I don't follow your analogy. I know that physical labor burns calories. What exactly does talking about a film do to the content of the film?

Sam: Talking about a film helps the viewer process it, work through it, understand it. The false philosophy in a film gets sorted out when viewers think through the film deeply, interpret it, and assess the film's worth.

Gibbs: How does talking through a filthy film make it safe? Perhaps I don't understand what it means for you to talk through a film. With whom did you "process" *The Wolf of Wall Street*?

Sam: I watched it with a few of the senior guys.

Gibbs: Not with your mother?

Sam: She's not a fan of Scorsese's work.

Gibbs: Is she not mature enough to handle his movies?

Sam: She doesn't know much about filmmaking, philosophy, or

those sorts of things.

Gibbs: She would find *The Wolf of Wall Street* confusing, in other words.

Sam: She would probably not want to sit through a film with quite so much strong content.

Gibbs: "Strong content"? Is she not a fan of profound dialogue, heady symbolism, and rich themes?

Sam: She does not like cursing.

Gibbs: I cannot imagine what else in *The Wolf of Wall Street* she would object to. Well, why don't you teach her how to handle such things?

Sam: It isn't in her temperament. My mother is very sentimental. She likes old black-and-white movies.

Gibbs: And your father?

Sam: My father has never been very interested in movies. He watches the news, *The Office*, and that's about it.

Gibbs: Does your pastor have an opinion on movies like *The Wolf of Wall Street*?

Sam: He's a pastor. Pastors have to tell you not to watch R-rated movies.

Gibbs: Well, if pastors have to say such things, you cannot possibly take them seriously. I probably don't need to ask about the idea of watching *The Wolf of Wall Street* with your grandparents.

Sam: Everyone's grandparents come from a more restrictive age. I doubt you asked your grandparents for their opinion of the music you listened to when you were a junior in high school.

Gibbs: Then who exactly are the older, wiser Christians that taught you to have deep philosophical conversations about filthy movies and thereby make them spiritually profitable?

Sam: I hear adults have deep philosophical conversations about stupid things all the time.

Gibbs: Fair enough. I am regularly amazed by the faith modern Christians place in "sitting down and talking things over." We really do have a bizarre confidence in the power of rational dialogue to create peace.

Sam: You don't think rational dialogue is the answer to most of our problems?

Gibbs: No.

Sam: Why not?

Gibbs: I suppose it is an occupational hazard. As a teacher of fifteen years, I have amassed entirely too much evidence to the contrary.

Sam: It is surprising to hear you say that. After all, you lecture for a living. You lead discussions among your students over abstract, difficult subjects. Your whole livelihood depends on talking things over.

Gibbs: Who better to understand the limited value of talking things over? I am not only a lecturer and a discussion leader but a judge of other people's children. I give Bs and Cs to children whose parents believe they are raising saints, geniuses, and scholars who could get a full ride to Oxford were it not for my small-minded, nitpicky, highly subjective claims about how mediocre Johnny's essays are. Most of the calm, rational conversations I have had with angry parents over the years have only made the situation worse.

Sam: What would you prefer? A fistfight? Should we resort to violence to sort out our differences?

Gibbs: People who believe that sitting down and talking things over is the best way of sorting out our problems also tend to believe it is the only way. If we are not talking, we will immediately begin fighting—or so it is thought. Maybe the reason we fight so much is because we can't be quiet. The desire to punch someone in the face who won't shut up is perfectly natural, even if it isn't a good idea.

Sam: Other than fighting and talking, what other way is there to solve our differences?

Gibbs: Silence. Bottling it all up. Not saying what you want to say. Stifling your feelings, shelving your thoughts and judgments. What else is there? There is patience. There is waiting. There is doing nothing.

Sam: Bottling it all up is dangerous.

Gibbs: Why?

Sam: You could blow.

Gibbs: People are more likely to blow in the middle of a "calm, rational conversation" with someone they despise than they are at home, alone and stewing. Silence requires more discipline, more sacrifice. Granted, carefully and coherently expressing your anger requires discipline, too; however, talking about things that make us angry rarely makes the anger subside. We often talk ourselves into new reasons for anger. We talk ourselves into deeper anger. It is not particularly surprising to me that divorce is so common in an era which believes the solution to every problem is a long, honest conversation. On occasions when my wife vexes and annoys me to the point that I want to confront her, the far better solution is simply to go to bed and wait for the joy which comes in the morning, as David describes in the Psalms. In the United States, the average marriage lasts eight years. Thus far, my marriage has lasted fifteen years. I credit the longevity of my marriage to our mutual willingness to say relatively little about our feelings.

Sam: So, you're against talking things over?

Gibbs: Not at all. I simply believe the modern man's confidence in talking things over is misplaced. Even when sitting down and talking "works," the real reconciliation is often accomplished in the days and weeks after the conversation is over. Passions cool, people forget, the business of life takes over, we move on. The age of social media has led to endless chatter about race and gender; nonetheless, I still regularly encounter people who claim, "Our problems with race will not go away until we can openly discuss them." The idea that we talk too much about race and gender is blasphemous. Americans used to believe that throwing enough money at a problem would make it go away. Today, we believe that throwing enough words at our problems is the answer. It is certainly pleasant to think our problems can be talked through, but if we are honest with ourselves, we will admit the idea is usually too good to be true. Talking is quick and easy. Granted, a "hard conversation" can feel a good bit like dying, but for the vast majority of the disagreements, complaints, irritations, insults, and indignations a man must suffer in his marriage and his church and his workplace, the most reliable solutions are prayer, confession, and good old-fashioned bottling-it-up while time wears away the rough edges of offense.

Sam: What does this have to do with movies?

Gibbs: It has everything in the world to do with movies. You boasted earlier of being able to think through tangled philosophical claims with a mature interpretive strategy. How can you not see the connection between marriage and movies?

Sam: Humor me. Given that you talk and write for a living, I would have thought you'd be pleased to know I write about film. In fact, I've heard you say there are some issues a man cannot understand until he writes about them. Would you prefer I simply watch a film and go to bed without saying a word about it?

ON GOOD TASTE

Gibbs: Yes.

Sam: Why?

Gibbs: What I mean is that you should watch a good film and go to bed. It is more important for you to watch good movies than it is for you to tear bad movies apart. At the moment, you imagine yourself to have this heroic, adversarial relationship with film. A film tries to deceive you, but you figure out all the angles, defeat the film, and then rifle through the film's pockets for anything valuable before moving on. This all seems very sophisticated to you, but it strikes me as tawdry. The fact that you're willing to watch films which demand such a viewing strategy means you don't know how to pick a movie. Simply put, you have terrible taste in film.

Sam: Would you agree that most Hollywood films are full of lies?

Gibbs: Of course, but I would also argue you ought to avoid most Hollywood films. If a film is deceptive and full of lies, skip it. Watch a good movie instead.

Sam: How do I know if a film is deceptive and full of lies until I watch it?

Gibbs: How do I know if a babysitter is pure and honest until she watches my young children?

Sam: Most people only hire babysitters they know or who have been recommended by a close friend.

Gibbs: Exactly. Likewise, you should watch films that are recommended to you by someone you trust. Watch classics from the 1940s and 1950s, films that are widely regarded as worthy of time and consideration. Watch films that older, wiser critics speak highly of. If you watch fewer movies overall and maintain a far higher standard for hitting "play," you will get a better return on your time.

Sam: Are classics not up for conversation after the credits roll?

Gibbs: The kind of conversation one has about a classic is entirely different from the conversation one has about a newly released film that isn't worth a second viewing. The sort of R-rated films that attract your attention because they seem grown-up and challenging aren't worth the level of examination you want to give them. If you're going to spend a long time mulling over a work of art, you ought to mull over good artwork.

Sam: At the beginning of this conversation, you implied that not all R-rated films are the same, but just now you referred to "the sort of R-rated films" that I like. We have only discussed one R-rated film. How do you know what kind of films I like?

Gibbs: One cannot talk about "R-rated films" without reducing films to their objectionable content. Christians who stick up for "R-rated films" typically exonerate the objectionable content because it is "real," or because the rest of the film is "culturally important." Christians who condemn "R-rated films" do so because, "I will set nothing wicked before my eyes," or some other hastily misapplied passage of Scripture. I am perfectly willing to recommend some very good films to you, and some are rated R, but the rating has nothing to do one way or another with why I would recommend them. I would tell you to watch a good movie because you need to see it, not because the movie needs you to pretend you understand it.

Sam: Am I not smart enough to understand a good movie?

Gibbs: No. Not on a first viewing. Neither am I, really. You might understand the basic outline of the plot, but a good work of art requires some time to mull over. If someone you trust recommends a film to you, though, you can turn off your brain when the film starts and simply take it all in. Likewise, if my dearest friend in the world recommended a certain babysitter for my children and said, "We leave our kids with her all the time," I would feel comfortable doing the same even though I had never met the babysitter before. I know the idea of turning off your brain before watching a film sounds like heresy given how many Christians endlessly chatter about the need to be constantly alert, always on guard, always judging, always ready to liken the latest fashionable rap album to the Gospel, always ready to show the subtle effects of Marxism on modern politics, always prepared to say something interesting about the latest event in the news cycle. However, a great work of art is capable of feeding your soul—if you have the humility to yield to it. Great art deserves to be treated very differently from tawdry art.

Sam: How does a great work of art "feed the soul"?

Gibbs: A great work of art is beautiful, and beauty is the food of the soul. Beauty serves no material function. It does not keep our hearts beating or our stomachs full. It does not keep the wind and rain out. The fact that we desire beauty even though it serves no material function is proof that a man is something other than mere material. Food, clothing, and shelter make life possible, but beauty makes life good. Beauty proves there is something beyond the material world, which is what makes it possible for the material world to have meaning. Because of beauty, the material world can refer to something beyond itself. When we receive beautiful things, we glimpse that higher, better world. We taste that world, breathe it in, hear its music. Once you understand that the point of art is beauty, not self-expression, the idea of watching crass films just to tear them apart seems an absurd waste of time.

Sam: How long does it take to understand something which is truly beautiful?

Gibbs: A long time, but the wait is not frustrating. When I was sixteen, I saw *Gattaca* in the theater and was undone by it. I told my friends the film was very good, but I had a hard time explaining why. Beauty often confounds us, stuns us into silence. We know that we ought to praise beautiful things, and yet beautiful things do not stand or fall on our praise. As testaments to a higher and better world, beautiful things are independent of us. A beautiful thing is even a little independent of its maker, which is why many artists claim they are carried along in the creative process by forces they cannot entirely control. It was not until I had seen *Gattaca* a dozen times that I got a handle on why I loved it.

Sam: You said you saw *Gattaca* in the theater. You did not know it would be great, but it was.

Gibbs: True. I have wasted a good bit of time and money watching new movies in the theater. For every *Gattaca* I have seen, there have been two dozen films like *Air Force One* and *Battlefield Earth*, which I also saw in the theater. The thing is, if I hadn't seen *Gattaca* in the theater, I would have seen it eventually because it has been recommended to me by people I trust many times over the years. I used to be the editor of a film review website. I have written close to a hundred movie reviews in the last ten years, but I think now that the only ones worth writing were for films I had seen many times and thought through deeply over a long period of time.

Sam: You think it was a waste of time to review new movies?

Gibbs: I do. You go to the theater and watch some dumb Liam Neeson action movie, then come home and do what? Figure out some way of teasing "It was a dumb Liam Neeson action movie, just like the trailer suggested" into 1200 words. Or what is more common these days: you watch a dumb comic book movie, then come home and figure out some way of referencing Heidegger, Lacan, and Foucault in the review, as though understanding a billion-dollar special effects bonanza requires a knowledge of post-structural philosophy.

Sam: There are some comic book movies that are actually quite sophisticated.

Gibbs: That is a claim which has arisen alongside the sale of comic book toys to adults—and not just comic book toys, but all kinds of toys. Bookstores are now full of action figures marketed to people in their thirties, but especially to men. References to esoteric philosophers in reviews of *Avengers* movies largely exist to placate the consciences of infantilized adults who still have teenage tastes.

Sam: That sounds like a different conversation.

Gibbs: If you say so.

Sam: What is *Gattaca* rated?

Gibbs: If someone finished watching *Gattaca* and immediately began complaining about the language and the sex, I would think that person a tasteless philistine. However, I think the decision to watch *The Wolf of Wall Street* equally tasteless, regardless of what brilliant comments are made about the film later.

Sam: Is that not a double standard? When a film you enjoy is concerned, objectionable content is of secondary importance, and yet when a film I enjoy is on the line, the objectionable content makes it "filthy."

Gibbs: Common sense has to be a criterion when choosing what we watch, what we listen to, what we read, and so forth. I would recommend *Gattaca* to my priest or to my mother. I don't feel the need to offer an acrobatic apology for why watching the film is morally allowable. Neither my friends, my family, my acquaintances, nor the people I work with would regard it as strange that I think *Gattaca* is a decent film, even if they do not care for the film personally.

Sam: That seems a bit relativistic.

Gibbs: If I were a relativist, I would say, "Whatever you feel is best for you is actually best for you." I'm not arguing anything of the kind. You are arguing that watching *The Wolf of Wall Street* is best for you, and I am arguing that you're being ridiculous.

Sam: You have not appealed to a universal standard. Based on your argument, I have no way of telling whether a movie is allowable or not. You think *Gattaca* is fine, but *The Wolf of Wall Street* isn't, though your criteria seem to be nothing better than, "What would other people say about it?" I certainly see quantitative differences between the films—there is more objectionable content in *The Wolf of Wall Street*—but not a difference of kind.

Gibbs: Common sense is largely considered with quantitative differences. If one man drinks a shot of whiskey and another man drinks a bottle of whiskey, you cannot argue the difference between them is merely quantitative, because one will be blind drunk and the other will not.

Sam: So, what standard governs whether a film is allowable to watch?

Gibbs: It seems like you are looking for some kind of equation whereby a film is reduced to a numerical quantity of objectionable content, divided by the total running time, and if the number is lower than two, it is permissible to watch.

Sam: At what point is there a sufficient amount of nudity or violence or vulgarity in a film that a Christian should not watch it?

Gibbs: I am contending you have terrible taste in film and that you don't know what movies are for—or why art even exists, really. I want you to watch good movies, and I have given you rather simple criteria for determining goodness. You should watch classic films from the

1940s and 1950s, films that have been praised and recommended for a good long time, films that you would not be embarrassed to recommend to your pastor or your mother. I'll throw the 1960s in for good measure. The fact a movie is clean is no justification for watching it because plenty of family-friendly films are banal and stupid. It's not as though I've been cryptic about how you ought to proceed. You seem to be under the impression that anything less than an abstract theory is relativistic, though.

Sam: Anything less than an abstract theory?

Gibbs: Your position seems to be, "Either all R-rated films are allowable, or else none are," and so the particular merits of a film do not matter because merits are debatable.

Sam: Don't you believe merits are debatable?

Gibbs: Of course.

Sam: Then you admit your standard for evaluating films is subjective?

Gibbs: Again, yes.

Sam: Then you are a relativist. Subjective standards are self-serving.

Gibbs: What do you think the word "subjective" means?

Sam: It is the opposite of "objective," which refers to transcendent truth or realities that are independent of our opinions. Opinions are subjective, which doesn't make them bad, but it does mean they cannot be used as standards.

Gibbs: Do all opinions have the same value?

Sam: All opinions are opinions.

Gibbs: All wine is wine. Does all wine have the same value?

Sam: All wine will get you drunk.

Gibbs: All love is love, as modern secularists like to say. Does all love have the same value?

Sam: That's different.

Gibbs: You seem to think that a firm faith in the ultimate importance of objectivity can save you from relativism, but in refusing to acknowledge the importance of subjectivity, you've begun to reason like a materialist. As Lewis put it somewhere, you have reduced what things are to what they are made of. You probably think stars are nothing but flaming balls of gas.

Sam: If you believe there are true opinions and false opinions, you do not understand what an opinion is.

Gibbs: I am surprised to hear a Christian like yourself reasoning like a secularist. Modern men often claim that the fact all opinions are unprovable means they are all basically the same; however, "I am entitled to my opinion," is a line of defense typically taken up by people who cannot defend their stupid opinions.

Sam: How can an opinion be stupid?

Gibbs: An opinion is not factual, but a good opinion is an elegant interpretation of facts. Elegance is not objective. You cannot purchase a pound of it. You cannot prove something is elegant in a court of law. You seem to think, though, that objective judgments and subjective judgments are naturally at odds with one another. In fact, responsible people ground their subjective judgments in objective realities. If two people see the same film and one says, "I thought it was good because…" and then elaborates for several minutes on the various merits of the plot, the soundtrack, the dialogue, and so forth, but the other person says, "I thought the film was terrible," but cannot explain why, the second person does not need to be taken all that seriously. If all opinions are equally meritorious, there really isn't any point to thinking deeply through something.

Sam: What you are arguing sounds kind of snobby.

Gibbs: Do you believe taste is relative, then? Is there no such thing as "good taste" or "bad taste"—only "my taste" and "your taste"?

Sam: I think you have too much confidence in the importance of good taste.

Gibbs: Why?

Sam: What is ultimately important is knowing the truth and believing the truth.

Gibbs: "You do well to say you believe there is one God. Even the demons believe and tremble" (James 2:19).

Sam: What are you arguing, then? Belief in God is not enough to get to heaven; a man must be able to appreciate an expensive wine, as well?

Gibbs: What exactly do you think "good taste" is?

Sam: I couldn't say, but I know that people who endlessly talk about good taste and insist on their own good taste are elitists and snobs.

Gibbs: There is a world of difference between people who talk about good taste and people who insist on their own good taste.

Sam: Prove it.

Gibbs: I talk about good taste quite a lot, but I would not claim to have good taste. I very much want to have good taste, but I don't have it yet.

Sam: Because you don't have the money for it.

Gibbs: So, you can say what good taste is?

Sam: I know it is a privilege of the rich.

Gibbs: Have you ever been to a library?

Sam: Of course.

Gibbs: And how much does it cost to check out a copy of *Fifty Shades of Gray* at a library?

Sam: It doesn't cost anything.

Gibbs: And how much does it cost to check out a copy of *Pride & Prejudice?*

Sam: Again, nothing.

Gibbs: Then good taste is not the exclusive province of the rich. Likewise, every modern library maintains a large collection of films, and it costs just as much to check out *Citizen Kane* as it does to check out an *Avengers* movie. It costs just as much to attend a traditional church which carries out dignified worship of God on Sunday mornings as it does to attend a worship center with a rock band and a motivational speaker who holds a Bible while he paces around the stage like Mick Jagger. Good taste comes to people who are willing to work for it.

Sam: How does one work for good taste?

Gibbs: By despairing of the shocking, sexy, spectacular works of art and culture that are wildly popular one year and gone the next.

Sam: In favor of what?

Gibbs: In favor of books and music and films which have lasted.

Sam: Why does lasting matter so much?

ON GOOD TASTE

Gibbs: Have you never wondered why people never tire of Beethoven? Have you never wondered why *It's a Wonderful Life* still runs in theaters all over the world every December? Why we still read *Paradise Lost* and Dante's *Divine Comedy* and Homer's *Odyssey*?

Sam: We read them because they're classics, and so they're important.

Gibbs: Why did they become classics?

Sam: I couldn't say.

Gibbs: Why is the most popular song of the year never the most popular song of the next year?

Sam: I suppose people get tired of it.

Gibbs: Why do they get tired of it?

Sam: Because they have heard it too often.

Gibbs: Why have they heard it too often?

Sam: Because it sounds good.

Gibbs: Why have we not tired of Beethoven?

Sam: People don't listen to Beethoven the way they listen to popular music.

Gibbs: You're onto something important. Explain the difference.

Sam: When a song is popular, people listen to it every day. Some people put popular songs on repeat and listen to them for hours.

Gibbs: We don't listen to certain songs every day just because they're popular.

Sam: No, we listen to those songs because they sound good.

Gibbs: Be more specific. What do you mean by "good"?

Sam: Songs become popular if they're catchy.

Gibbs: Or amusing, clever, sexy, exciting, or shocking.

Sam: Those aren't the only reasons.

Gibbs: No, but they are the most common ways for determining whether a work of art is going to be wildly popular. The problem, though, is that none of those qualities lasts all that long.

Sam: I disagree. People have always liked clever things. Clever isn't going anywhere. Neither is sexy, for that matter.

Gibbs: You haven't grasped my point. What counts as sexy changes rather quickly. What was thought sexy back in the 1980s looks very silly today. The kind of clothing that marked a woman out as a prostitute in the 1940s would make a modern woman look like a chaste homemaker. The same is true of movies which promised "big thrills" fifty years ago. We are quite bored by them now. A film has to offer something other than thrills in order to last.

Sam: But that's because technology has improved. We demand better special effects over time for the same reason we demand better gas mileage from cars over time.

Gibbs: If a film is ultimately discarded simply because technology has improved, it was never much of a film to begin with. It was really more of a toaster.

Sam: Then why do some things last?

Gibbs: Beautiful things last. Good and true things last. Goodness is not a quality that can be adjusted by turning a dial. Loud things are exciting, but it does not take skill or genius to make music louder. Fast things are exciting, but a modern music producer can make music faster just by pushing a button. Sexy things are exciting; however, trimming a few more inches off the hem of a skirt is simple and easy. When the popularity of a work of art is entirely based on the fact it is exciting or thrilling, it won't last because someone will come along the following year and turn the dial up a little higher. There is no dial that makes a book like *Jane Eyre* more brilliant, though. Trimming a few inches off a lady's skirt might make her sexier, but it does not make her more beautiful. Beautiful, true, and good things are very rare. They are so rare, in fact, that reasonable people hold on tightly to them whenever they come along. That is why they last.

Sam: I understand your point, and I think I agree, but I also think there is something important missing from your theory of taste. I just can't quite put my finger on it.

Gibbs: You may have inadvertently answered your own question.

The view of art and taste I have put forward is quite literally missing something important. So much modern art—modern music, modern film, modern fiction—is marketed as being "very important."

Sam: That is true. Over the last ten years, more and more films have self-consciously included elements of race or gender in the plot or the casting. Such films are always advertised as being "very important."

Gibbs: It really does not take much for a modern film or novel to be touted as "very important." It merely needs to reference some fashionable political cause. However, when everything is very important, nothing is. Everything which is important today is replaced by something even more important tomorrow. While we have no standard for importance at all, importance has effectively replaced goodness and beauty as the preeminent quality we look for in a thing. The modern company gave up advertising the quality of its product some time ago. Now, the modern company advertises its own importance—and obeying the most current standards of ethics is the most important thing there is.

Sam: Is *Jane Eyre* important, though? Is *It's a Wonderful Life* important?

Gibbs: Of course. But the importance of *It's a Wonderful Life* is entirely based on the goodness of the film. Because the film is good, many different kinds of people have seen it. Old people, young people. Black people, white people. Rich people, poor people. It's a common reference point across four generations and it doesn't show any sign of going away. The modern standard of importance is merely "what people like me are talking about today." Truly important things don't have to advertise the fact they are important. Likewise, anything that is truly world-famous doesn't need to tell you it is "world-famous." There are only three things in the world that are actually world-famous: Coca-Cola, Catholicism, and Marlboro cigarettes. But you don't see signs outside the Chartres Cathedral saying, "Come pray to the world-famous Virgin Mary." Everybody knows the deal.

Sam: Let me be honest with you. I just don't enjoy the sorts of very old, very good things you're talking about.

Gibbs: I know. As someone who was raised on a heavy diet of popular culture, it is hard for me to enjoy them, as well. That is why I told you I want to have good taste, although I don't have it yet.

Sam: What is good taste?

Gibbs: Good taste is a taste for good things. Good taste is the enjoyment of good things—which doesn't come naturally. It is a skill, an ability. It has to be learned. I would say it has to be earned, as well.

Sam: How is it earned?

Gibbs: Through discipline. Through forcing yourself to listen to good music—which is demanding and sophisticated and ultimately rewarding—even though you would rather listen to pleasant music which asks nothing of you. Good taste in anything—food, art, fiction—means many years of yielding and submitting to good things. Simple, foolish things can be dominated. This is one of the reasons you like the sort of movies you do. You can push them around. You cannot push good things around, though. It is pointless. Good things don't need you. You need them. We earn good taste through the discipline of resisting things that are immediately pleasant in favor of things that slowly become pleasant. Without beauty, we would all be slaves of our most immediate physical desires.

Sam: And this is why good taste is not simply a negligible matter of opinion.

Gibbs: That is correct. In the same way that good things last, good taste lasts. If you learn to love good things when you are young, you can take those loves with you into adulthood and into old age. The man who follows his immediate physical desires never loves anything for very long. Bad taste makes a man shallow and shallow people cannot be trusted.

Sam: Bad taste could quickly sink a marriage, then.

Gibbs: How do you figure?

Sam: If a man only follows his most immediate physical desires, he won't be capable of maintaining a long-term relationship with a woman. If he only loves things that are easy to love, his love won't outlast a difficult year of marriage.

Gibbs: Agreed. It is easy to love someone who is young, beautiful, and has relatively few responsibilities. As a marriage goes on, though, a couple slowly accrues greater responsibilities, which means greater opportunities for failure and disappointment. A young married couple can devote an astounding amount of their time and energy directly to one another. In the tenth year of marriage, though, the husband and wife love one another by taking care of the kids, the bills, the lawn, and so forth. This indirect form of love is less physically pleasant, but far more interesting and intellectually satisfying, at least for people with strong minds. Weak-minded people think a marriage has lost its reason for existing once it ceases to be pleasant. Such a conclusion invariably results from bad taste, which not only involves the love of pleasure, but usually involves an inability to love anything for very long.

Sam: Is it possible to develop a long-term relationship with bad art?

Gibbs: Yes, but I don't think such relationships are all that common. Bad things aren't worth suffering for, which means we have little incentive to remain true to bad things when the going gets tough.

Sam: What do you mean by "when the going gets tough"?

Gibbs: When bad things bore us, we guiltlessly abandon them. When bad things become unfashionable, we have little reason to stick up for them. When bad things cease to please us, we feel no obligation to find new ways to interpret them so they become pleasing again. It is the goodness of good things that compels our faithfulness to them. We have reason to believe that good things are worth the struggle to attain them—this is simply what "goodness" means. We have obligations to good things, which means it is possible to fail good things. It is not possible to fail something that exists solely for your pleasure. For this reason, many people resolve to "try to get into music," but no one makes a new year's resolution to learn to like pop music. If a pop song does not please you, it is the song which has failed, not you.

Sam: You have used the word "obligation" several times now, but I don't understand how it is possible to have an obligation to Handel's *Messiah*.

Gibbs: You're entirely right. When I say we have an obligation to good things, I mean we have an obligation to the people who, over the centuries, have had the discipline to perpetuate good things. The *Messiah* is around now because people listened to the *Messiah* twenty-five years ago, fifty years ago, seventy-five years ago, and so on. If an entire generation completely gives up on the *Messiah*, there is a good chance it would be lost completely.

Sam: But why? How? It could still be rediscovered.

Gibbs: I don't mean that every recording of the *Messiah* would suddenly vanish into thin air. However, the love of good things is something most people must learn from others, which means that unless someone tells you to listen to the *Messiah*, there is not much chance you will seek it out on your own.

Sam: So a man learns good taste from someone older than himself? And that older person learned good taste from someone older still?

Gibbs: Yes.

Sam: This almost sounds like the Catholic doctrine of apostolic succession.

Gibbs: A fascinating analogy. Hopefully this explanation accounts for the highly personal element of good taste we were discussing earlier—which sounded like relativism to you before.

Sam: No, I understand it now. A student is not above his teacher.

Gibbs: But every student, when fully formed, becomes like his teacher.

DIALOGUE 6

On College

Oliver: In class, you talk a lot about the temptations which come with college. How did you do in college?

Gibbs: Not very well. I dropped out three times and it took me ten years to graduate with a bachelor's degree. If I had it to do over again, I would do college very differently.

Oliver: Occasionally I hear about graduates from this school going off the rails in college.

Gibbs: So do I.

Oliver: Why do you think some students go off the rails and others don't?

Gibbs: Let me offer you three very basic rules for not losing your head in college. First, go to church. Second, go to class. Third, call your dad. Most students who go off the rails in college fail to do at least one of these three things.

Oliver: Why not, "Don't do drugs"? Or "Don't sleep around"? Doesn't "going off the rails" in college typically mean drugs and promiscuity?

Gibbs: Sure, but Christian kids usually don't show up at college and immediately start doing drugs and sleeping around. They have to work up to those vices, which typically means quitting church, skipping class, and rarely checking in back home.

Oliver: Why is skipping class such a big deal? If attendance isn't required in a class, and the class isn't that great, isn't skipping it simply a matter of prudence?

Gibbs: The first time you skip class, nothing bad will happen, and so you will only be emboldened to do it again. Skipping class is slippery, though, and it's a habit that will quickly get away from you. Take note of the reasons why you skip class, or why others do so. There's rarely a good reason. The reason is usually no better than, "I don't want to go." Or you manage your time badly and need to finish something which could have been done the previous night. Skipping class is a good way of forgetting why you're even going to college.

Oliver: Why am I going to college?

Gibbs: Either to learn virtue or to get a job. Either way, skipping class is bad juju.

Oliver: Why? If I can still do well in a class, does it matter if I skip?

Gibbs: In and of itself, getting good grades in college means very little. If you want to get something out of college, you need to go to class every day, sit in the front row, and know something about what the professor does outside of class. This means being able to say, "Hey, Stephen, really interesting article on *Huffington Post* last week." That is how you win the respect of the teacher, how you get nominated for departmental prizes, how you get strong letters of recommendation.

Oliver: I don't have to study? I don't have to be brilliant?

Gibbs: I have been giving students this advice for years and I have yet to hear of anyone actually taking it. Most students arrive at college and quickly figure out which classes repay attendance and which ones don't, but by that point, it's all over for you. You fell for the good grades trap. If you want to start getting over the good grades trap now, look around this school, figure out which teacher leads the happiest, best life, and then start following that teacher around everywhere. Ask him what he thinks about taxes and birth control and the Academy Awards. Ask him what he does on Saturdays, what he reads to his kids, what he buys his wife for her birthday, what his favorite Beatles song is. That will get you somewhere. What won't get you somewhere? Getting good grades and "just wanting to be left alone" won't get you anywhere.

Oliver: Perhaps someone who skips class is not going to get nominated for departmental prizes, but when this conversation began, we were discussing how to not go off the rails in college.

Gibbs: Yes, and when a fellow forgets why he is going to college in the first place, going off the rails happens rather easily.

Oliver: Why?

Gibbs: When you forget that you have come to college to learn virtue and to get a job, your friends quickly become your reason for being in college—and those friends have started skipping classes, too.

Oliver: But friends are important. Community is important.

Gibbs: Were you under the impression that spending a lot of time with your friends in college was going to keep you from going off the rails?

Oliver: Can't good friends keep you from going off the rails?

Gibbs: Quite a few people go off the rails because they depend too much on their friends to keep them on the straight and narrow. In the last four years, how often have your friends kept you from doing something dumb? How many times have your friends confronted you on your sin? It is against school rules to have a cell phone on your person throughout the day, but how many times have you told someone looking at their cell phone in the restroom to put it away?

Oliver: I think you undervalue the importance of friends.

Gibbs: What would overvaluing the importance of friends look like?

Oliver: I don't think you can overvalue the importance of friends.

ON COLLEGE

Gibbs: Very good. That kind of statement is exactly what overvaluing the importance of friends looks like.

Oliver: No, I actually meant what I said. I really don't think the importance of friendship can be overvalued.

Gibbs: Oh, I see. That is typically the kind of sentiment that leads a Christian college student to quit going to church.

Oliver: Why?

Gibbs: Where do you go to church now?

Oliver: My family attends a PCA church.

Gibbs: If you move away for college, there is a good chance none of your new friends will attend a PCA church.

Oliver: So?

Gibbs: Are you willing to attend a church where you don't know anybody?

Oliver: I won't need to do that. When I make new friends in college, I can worship wherever they worship.

Gibbs: If you move away for college, you should commit yourself as quickly as possible to whatever PCA church there is in town, even if they do not have a singles group, even if you do not like the music, even if the pastor is too dull or too cool for your taste. If you only go to a certain church because your friends go there, you will quit going to church rather quickly.

Oliver: Why?

Gibbs: Because eventually your friends will quit going to church.

Oliver: That is rather pessimistic. Why are my friends going to quit going to church?

Gibbs: Because they will get jobs and have to work on Sundays. Or they will take road trips to New York or Boston for the weekend. Or they will simply be too tired or else have papers to write. Or they will begin looking for new churches, which is the fast track to apostasy. Christian kids who are new to college do not quit going to church in protest or because they suddenly come to doubt the existence of God. They quit going because of sloth and laziness and because the worries of life overwhelm them. Going to church reminds you what you are and what you must therefore do. When you have not been to church in a year, you forget these things. It is far easier to do things Pastor Steve does not approve of when you have not seen Pastor Steve since last October.

Oliver: What if I want to look around a bit before deciding which church to attend?

Gibbs: Pick one church to attend on Sunday mornings. Do your looking around on Wednesday nights and Sunday nights. Going to church twice a week will help balance out the inherent dangers of shopping for churches.

ON COLLEGE

Oliver: That seems a bit drastic.

Gibbs: If you want to keep your head in college, you will need to take drastic action.

Oliver: I see.

Gibbs: Attending a PCA church in college will also scale back the possibility that you will gutlessly bow down and worship the zeitgeist.

Oliver: What?

Gibbs: While drugs and promiscuity represent a sad capitulation to what both St. Paul and Jesus Christ commonly refer to as "the world," there are other ways of becoming the world's stooge. I am just as vexed when my students, who have studied beauty and truth, graduate high school and suddenly adopt trendy opinions on beauty, art, gender, marriage, politics, and so forth.

Oliver: You mean you don't like it when conservative students go liberal in college?

Gibbs: There are plenty of self-professed conservatives who fawningly serve the zeitgeist, as well.

Oliver: Admit it. It galls you to see your students veer left in college.

Gibbs: When I was in my twenties, I said an awful lot of foolish things to my elders, and now that I am nearly forty, people in their twenties say those kinds of things to me. Several months ago, a college sophomore spent twenty minutes trying to persuade me that it was actually important for Christians to understand *Transformers* as "a revealing work of social commentary." However, I would regularly bore adults with the same kind of pablum back when I was in college. There was a movement called "the emergent church" which was quite popular back when I was in my twenties, and I was a little entranced by it for a while. One of the central figures in the emergent church movement was this fellow who would do stuff like wear a Mickey Mouse shirt while he preached and reference emo songs in his sermons. I used to think that was pretty cutting-edge stuff.

Oliver: And you are just so above it now, huh?

Gibbs: I spent my twenties regretting my teens. I have spent my thirties regretting my twenties. It is not hard to guess what I will be doing in my forties.

Oliver: Does it really matter if a guy wears a Mickey Mouse T-shirt if he is preaching the Gospel? This just brings me around to my original question, though. If the teachers at this school cared less about little stuff like how students dress, and what music we play at school parties and sporting events, and cared more about the Gospel, maybe students wouldn't quit the faith in college.

Gibbs: What do you think became of the Mickey Mouse preacher?

Oliver: I bet he is still preaching the Gospel.

Gibbs: Okay.

ON COLLEGE

Oliver: So, a conservative kid goes off to college, realizes that liberals have a few decent ideas, and then he gives his life over to sex, drugs, and rock 'n' roll?

Gibbs: Not exactly. College tends to create an optical illusion which leads many students to believe they are in a better place to judge their parents than they actually are, and as soon as you're dismissing the politics of your parents, dismissing their morality becomes much easier, as well.

Oliver: What's the optical illusion?

Gibbs: That you are taking care of yourself and so you're entitled to a few opinions of your own.

Oliver: Isn't a college student taking care of himself?

Gibbs: An acrobat who is embarrassed to admit he uses a safety net nonetheless acts more boldly because he knows it is there.

Oliver: I don't get it.

Gibbs: In college, you have to feed yourself, dress yourself, take yourself to the doctor if you get sick. At the same time, this isn't really self-sufficiency. You will continue to depend on your parents for money, for the underwriting of loans, for cell phone bills, for emergencies, for Christmas presents and birthday presents which substantially contribute to your well-being, and for room and board three or four months out of the year. Nonetheless, when a college student feeds himself and dresses himself, he will be tempted to also say, "I take care of myself, so I should think for myself, too," and feel it necessary to begin disagreeing with his parents on politics, which will quickly lead to disagreements about morality, as well.

Oliver: So, a college student has to believe everything his parents say?

Gibbs: That's not a bad idea. In the *Analects,* Confucius says that after his father dies, a wise son changes nothing about the estate he inherits for three whole years. I believe that. When you go to college, work hard, work more, pray more, but hold off on the temptation to radically reinvent yourself.

Oliver: Is that why you think college students should call their parents?

Gibbs: I think young men should call their fathers often, yes.

Oliver: What good will that do?

Gibbs: It will be a reminder of just how much you are doing that you shouldn't be. When you call your father, your father will say, "How's it going, son?" and if you've been fooling around with girls and smoking dope and skipping class, you can always just lie to your father, but lying to him will clarify for you just what kind of person you're becoming. You're becoming the kind of person who cannot be honest with the people who love you.

Oliver: That's kind of a grim reason to call your parents.

Gibbs: I know.

Oliver: Is that really the only reason I should call my dad when I go to college? So I feel guilty about lying about all the bad things I've done?

Gibbs: It's not as though you want to talk to him. I am trying to give you a good and pious reason to call home.

Oliver: How about because I love him?

Gibbs: Is that reason sufficient right now to compel you to talk to him for more than ten minutes a week?

Oliver: I mean—

Gibbs: If you don't talk to your dad for more than ten minutes a week now, you're not going to start doing it once you go off to college. Look, of all the Christian kids you've heard about going off the rails in college, how many were male?

Oliver: Most of them.

Gibbs: Had you realized that before this moment?

Oliver: No.

Gibbs: It's hard to be young, male, and free to stay up as late as you want. You've got a sister, don't you?

Oliver: Yes.

Gibbs: And she talks to your mother far more than you talk to your father, am I right?

Oliver: Well, yes.

Gibbs: For kids not raised in the church, the college vice squad is an equal opportunity employer. For kids raised in the church, the vice squad is far harder on young men. You need a plan to fight that kind of temptation. Your twenties are a very difficult time to keep your faith in God. You cannot simply cross your fingers and hope everything turns out well. You need a plan.

Oliver: What makes your twenties so difficult?

Gibbs: Not just your twenties, but the few years which come right before your twenties, as well. Generally speaking, very few people do well when they suddenly move from a controlled, stable environment into a condition of near total freedom, autonomy, and anonymity. Right now, your parents bring God near to you—I mean they physically bring Him near to you. They take you to church whether you want to go or not. They lead you in prayer. They keep Bibles around. Your mother writes Bible verses on index cards and tapes them around the kitchen. The very presence of your parents reminds you that telling lies and stealing are wrong. When you are no longer near your parents, there is no one who reliably brings God near to you. You must bring yourself near to God, which is hard to do.

Oliver: But I love God.

Gibbs: Thus far, your parents have made it easy for you to love Him. When you move away to college, loving God becomes far more difficult.

Oliver: Why?

Gibbs: Because God is hard to love.

Oliver: Why?

Gibbs: Because you can't see Him. St. John asks rhetorically how any man can claim to love God, Whom he cannot see, when he does not love his brother, whom he can see. He simply assumes that human beings are far easier to love than God.

Oliver: Why does the fact we can't see God make Him harder to love?

Gibbs: That is a very important question. I am genuinely impressed you asked it. Most people simply leave St. John's assertion alone; it rings true and that is good enough. The sort of love people want when they are young is very different than the sort of love they come to appreciate when they grow old. At seventeen, the sort of love a girlfriend gives is direct, unambiguous, unmistakable. She tells you that she loves you, she admires you, she comes to your games, she holds your hand, she kisses your cheek. The love you give her is just as direct. You buy her gifts, take her out, tell her she is beautiful. However, when a relationship entirely centers around visible, obvious expressions of love, it just doesn't matter all that much.

Oliver: What do you mean it "doesn't matter"?

Gibbs: I mean the relationship exists for its own sake. It exists to make the people in the relationship feel good and feeling good simply isn't all that important. For this reason, when married people hear that some young couple is no longer dating, they typically don't feel all that much sympathy for the newly broken-hearted. When a married couple with three kids announces they are divorcing, their friends look on with sadness, sobriety, and self-reflection. It's a bit like seeing some diner that has been around since the 1960s finally closing its doors. When a dating couple breaks up, it's like hearing a Burger King is closing for a month to remodel.

Oliver: Doesn't marriage exist to make the husband and wife feel good?

Gibbs: No, marriage does not exist for that reason.

Oliver: Are you not happy with your marriage?

Gibbs: I'm very happy with my marriage, but that is only because my own happiness is not the point of my marriage.

Oliver: What's the point of your marriage?

Gibbs: Raising my children in the Christian faith. My own salvation and sanctification. The creation of a stable and productive family that will help my church and my community be stable and productive, as well. My wife is also my companion, of course, and we chose one another as companions because we are somewhat like-minded, enjoy the same things, and all the rest.... But productivity is far more important than good feelings. If my marriage existed primarily for the sake of my own good feelings, I would never accomplish anything.

Oliver: I suppose I'm a bit more romantic than you are. I plan on buying my wife flowers every Friday, writing her poems, getting her name tattooed on my chest, and "all the rest," as you put it.

Gibbs: If you want your marriage to last, you will have to worry about loving your wife in other ways, as well.

Oliver: I plan on bringing home a good paycheck.

Gibbs: Of course, but you will have to learn to receive love indirectly, as well.

Oliver: What do you mean?

Gibbs: Direct love is gift-giving, hand-holding, and compliments. Indirect love means not allowing your children to watch television all day because it will turn them into unhappy, disobedient brats— which, in turn, will inspire you to work longer hours than you need and inspire your wife to turn half-hour errands into two-hour errands so she can enjoy a little peace and quiet. Indirect love is what creates a stable enough marriage that you even want to give one another direct love. Direct love is intoxicating, though, and really so pleasant that it often numbs the intellect. A good deal of the love God has to offer is indirect, though, which is vexing to people in their twenties.

Oliver: And that's why they quit going to church?

Gibbs: Yes, they say they feel "far from God." On the other hand, many young people try to make up for that distance from God by making their relationship with Him as direct as possible, which is why young people enjoy romantic, erotic forms of worship at church. Really, though, such worship exists merely to give the worshipper good feelings. It is not productive; it is not stable, and this becomes obvious to many young people after a few years, at which point they give up on church.

Oliver: Shouldn't worship make you feel good, though?

Gibbs: As with marriage, the point of worship is not to make anyone feel good. If your heart is pure and your soul is unblemished, then I suppose worship would make you feel good; however, if you are not terribly interested in reading your Bible, praying, fasting, and giving to the poor, I suspect worship will make you a bit uncomfortable. It makes me uncomfortable. To be honest, I am always a bit relieved when church lets out.

Oliver: Then why do you keep going back?

Gibbs: The relief I feel when church lets out is exactly what keeps me coming back. It lets me know that I need to come back—that I must come back.

Oliver: And what if you someday experienced disappointment when church was over?

Gibbs: If I loved church so much that I was disappointed when it was over, I would obviously keep coming back to church. What sane person wouldn't? My point is this: I go to church because I need to, not because I want to, and certainly not because it makes me feel good. You need to go to a church that you need to go to. Want matters very little. But this is exactly why you should commit to the PCA church in whatever town you move to after college. If you allow a committee of your friends—who are no smarter than you—to choose where you go to church, you will choose some fashionable church that excites you today and bores you tomorrow, a church incapable of commanding your respect.

Oliver: But don't people need to feel at home at church?

Gibbs: Do they? How do you feel at home? Do you enjoy spending time with your parents, or do you look for excuses to be out of the house as often as possible?

Oliver: Fair enough.

Gibbs: Be willing to admit that feelings are unreliable, fickle, and not a solid groundwork for justifying anything. Feelings are not bad, but disconnected from reason, tradition, and common sense, feelings will steer you into jail. Your goal should not be finding a church which offers worship that makes you feel good. Your goal should be to sanctify your heart and mind, refine your tastes, and live your life so that the worship offered by your church is satisfying to your soul—but assume the sanctifying and refining will take some time.

Oliver: What if my parents attended the sort of church you're criticizing, though? If you're going to criticize churches that offer romantic worship, what would you tell me if my family attended that sort of church now?

Gibbs: If that were the case, I would still tell you to begin attending the same sort of church wherever you went. If you're going to look for another church, do it on Wednesday nights or Sunday nights. Wherever you go to church in college, you need a group of people expecting you to show up on Sunday morning. If you decide not to go to church on Sunday morning, you need a group of people who will call you to make sure you're okay. If you decide to switch your membership from one church to another, you need a new group of people expecting you on Sunday morning. You need to set yourself up for embarrassment and pointed questions if you don't make it to church—and if you choose a certain church just because your friends go there, they won't ask you pointed questions for sleeping in or "being too busy with school work to make it." That's not how friends work. Friends are too understanding. If you choose some boring little PCA church that only has ninety members, though, you're going to stick out like a sore thumb and attract the attention of people older than you—moms, dads, grandmothers who are going to tell you, "Come next week and I'll bring you some of my chicken soup." That's exactly what you need. Besides, you'll see your friends plenty during the week. Choosing a church your friends don't attend is pretty much the only way you're going to keep stable, responsible people part of your life.

Oliver: Why does your advice sound so different from all the other advice I've gotten about going to college?

ON COLLEGE

Gibbs: What sort of advice have other people given you?

Oliver: They all say, "It is very important to make good Christian friends in college."

Gibbs: How banal. That is simply not a plan for negotiating four years of freedom and sexual temptation. Your friends in college will not do more for your faith than your friends in high school do now.

Oliver: Granted, my friends are not doing a lot for my faith, but they are not exactly harming it, either.

Gibbs: That is because their parents bring God near to them, just as your parents bring God near to you. In college, not only will you suffer because your parents are far from you; you will suffer because your friends' parents are far from them, as well. But bring your father as near to you as you can. Call him often. Go to class so that you do not have to lie to him when you talk, because he will definitely ask if you have been going to class. The more you have to lie to your father, the less you will want to talk to him.

Oliver: What bleak advice.

Gibbs: Yes, for a bleak time of life.

DIALOGUE 7

Lead Me into Temptation

Thomasina: I am thinking of switching to a public school next year.

Gibbs: I see. Why is that?

Thomasina: I don't think I'm being challenged in my faith at this school. I'm worried that I'm just going along with the crowd here, just going through the motions. It's easy to be a Christian here. Everyone at this school is rather passive about their faith, and I'm afraid I will turn out the same.

Gibbs: What does it mean to be "challenged in your faith"?

Thomasina: I don't think my faith in God is growing deeper here. I want it to grow deeper.

Gibbs: Why don't you just get rid of your phone?

Thomasina: Why would I do that?

Gibbs: Without your phone, you would have to rely more on God than you do now. Without a phone, you would become something of an outsider at this school. You would be excluded and miss out on quite a lot. This would let you connect with other outcasts, befriend them, and help them. Also, you would waste far less time texting and scrolling through Instagram. If you got rid of your phone, you would probably end up praying more and reading your Bible more, too.

Thomasina: But having a phone is not necessarily bad, though.

Gibbs: Is your phone helping your faith in God grow deeper?

Thomasina: Not really.

Gibbs: So your phone is an impediment to your faith?

Thomasina: I guess.

Gibbs: And yet you don't get rid of it? It does not sound like you respond all that well when your faith is challenged. I would not recommend going to a public school next year.

Thomasina: So whether I should go to public school or not is dependent on whether I have a cell phone? By that rationale, everyone should have gone to public school twenty years ago.

Gibbs: A moment ago, you suggested that you wanted your faith in God to grow deeper. What ways have you tried to deepen your faith while at this school?

Thomasina: I can't just snap my fingers and deepen my faith. It doesn't work like that.

Gibbs: True. How often do you read your Bible?

Thomasina: Being a Christian isn't all about going to church and reading your Bible. Going to church doesn't make you a Christian. There's more. It means having a deep relationship with God.

Gibbs: Agreed. Nonetheless, how often?

Thomasina: Not as often as I should.

Gibbs: Why not?

Thomasina: Probably the same reason you don't read your Bible very often.

Gibbs: Touché. I do not read my Bible very often. Then again, I'm not the one who said I wanted my faith to be challenged.

Thomasina: Why not? Why don't you want your faith to be challenged?

Gibbs: Because my faith is weak.

Thomasina: If your faith were challenged, maybe it wouldn't be weak.

Gibbs: If my faith were challenged, it might wither up and die. If I make it into heaven, St. Peter is going to be stamping out a fire on the back of my robe.

Thomasina: My faith isn't weak, though.

Gibbs: Praise God. What makes you say that?

Thomasina: When I pray, I feel God's presence. I love singing to Him at church or in the car. There's this amazing quote from the runner Eric Liddell: "When I run, I feel God's pleasure." Running was like going to church for him. It was like worship. I feel God's pleasure when I share the Gospel. But I also feel God's pleasure when I'm just reading or going for a walk.

Gibbs: It sounds as though you're already quite close to God. If your faith is strong, it doesn't need a challenge. If your faith is weak, it cannot stand a challenge. I simply don't see why anyone should seek out a challenge to their faith.

Thomasina: Maybe "challenge" was the wrong word. Perhaps "exercise" is better. I want my faith to go to boot camp, toughen up, grow some endurance. There is nothing to endure at this school.

Gibbs: Maybe you could help your friends endure their problems. Perhaps that is why you are here.

Thomasina: See, that's the thing. I'm not like the students who go here, and so I don't really have close friends.

Gibbs: There is the solution to your problem. Not having friends is the exercise your faith needs. Isn't that something difficult for you to endure? Doesn't a lack of friends mean you have to rely more on God?

Thomasina: I mean, there are things to endure at this school, but those things are not drawing me closer to God.

Gibbs: Could they?

Thomasina: I suppose. But, let me just lay all my cards out here. I have always been drawn to missions work.

Gibbs: What does that mean?

Thomasina: I have always wanted to share the Gospel.

Gibbs: Share the Gospel with the students at this school. Trust me. They need it.

Thomasina: But most of the students don't need to hear the Gospel. They're not the unreached.

Gibbs: How do you know?

Thomasina: I mean, most of them already go to church.

Gibbs: A moment ago you said that going to church doesn't necessarily make someone a Christian. So maybe there are church-going students here who still need to hear the Gospel.

Thomasina: It is starting to seem like you just don't think I can handle it.

Gibbs: What do you mean "handle it"?

Thomasina: You think I'm going to lose my faith if I go to public school.

Gibbs: Do you think there are Christian kids who lose their faith in public school?

Thomasina: Yes, but there are Christian kids who lose their faith at private Christian schools, too.

Gibbs: That is definitely true.

Thomasina: So, you understand the danger?

Gibbs: Yes, a private Christian school is a place where many students face spiritual challenges.

Thomasina: Very funny. So, what is the difference between public schools and Christian schools? You act like they are similar when it suits your argument, but you act like they are totally different when it suits my argument. Are Christian schools and public schools similar or not?

Gibbs: No, they are not very similar.

Thomasina: Well, if I could lose my faith here or in public school, how are they different?

Gibbs: What you think of as "challenges" to your faith, I would simply call "temptations," and we are called to pray every day that God would not lead us into temptation. Are there not enough temptations in your life that you must seek out more?

Thomasina: Aren't we supposed to "do difficult things," though? Have I not heard teachers at this school give that piece of advice a dozen times this year?

Gibbs: Getting rid of your phone would be difficult, and it would call for an increase in your reliance on God, which would mean praying more. It is difficult to read your Bible, so you do not do it, nor do I. You might also try fasting—which I also rarely do—or you could give your pocket money to the poor. Any of these things might loosen the grip you have on this world and allow you to draw closer to God. Prayer, fasting, and almsgiving are the holy works Christ calls us to undertake, and He carefully explains how to do them in the Sermon on the Mount.

Thomasina: But Christ also says we should go into all nations and make disciples.

Gibbs: Yes. That's what I think of myself doing at this school. Making disciples.

Thomasina: So, if we're supposed to go to all nations and make disciples, shouldn't we go to all schools and make disciples, too?

Gibbs: Before I answer that question, let me ask you this: How well do you actually know the Gospel? How well do you know the Gospel story? How well versed are you in sound doctrine?

Thomasina: I know the Gospel story. Every Christian does. Jesus came to earth to—

Gibbs: Can you name all twelve apostles?

Thomasina: No, but what does that have to do with Jesus being crucified for our sins? Being a missionary is not about reading big thick theology books front to back. It is about being passionate for God's truth. If you know the basics of the Gospel, the Holy Spirit can make up for what you don't know. The Holy Spirit works in every presentation of the Gospel.

Gibbs: Interesting. So why do you need to enroll in a public school in order to make disciples there?

Thomasina: So I can become friends with the students and share the Gospel with them.

Gibbs: Why don't you just show up at football games and preach the Gospel to the students in the stands? You could drive over to the public schools in the afternoon, as well, and preach in the parking lots and on the sidewalks.

Thomasina: That would not work. People today don't take that kind of thing seriously. I would look insane.

Gibbs: But the Holy Spirit works in every presentation of the Gospel, as you just said. You don't need to enroll in a public school and make friends with everyone there before you can present the Gospel. That's an approach that's centered around you, not your message. Why don't you continue going to this school and simply preach the Gospel in the parking lot outside public school football games while students are walking in? God will work through your passion, won't He?

Thomasina: I don't like this school. It isn't a good fit.

Gibbs: Christians with very strong faith generally don't fit anywhere in the world. They are not residents here, but strangers and aliens.

Thomasina: Now you are just being coy.

Gibbs: If you would like a little advice that isn't coy, here it is: Christ prepared to be tempted by Satan by fasting in the wilderness for forty days. He cut himself off from the world and drew close to God. If you go to public school, you will enter into far greater temptation than you have here. I could fully endorse your choice to go to public school if you were willing to prepare for it. Give up your phone for a year. If you still wanted to go to public school after that time, I would fully endorse your venture.

Thomasina: You don't think I will, do you?

Gibbs: It is hard to say. God is full of surprises, and you are not, though God can work through you.

Thomasina: You must be the only adult I know who actively discourages people from sharing the Gospel.

Gibbs: This school desperately needs students who are willing to share the Gospel—not with students from the public school, but with students from this school.

Thomasina: You have implied that before, but who exactly are you talking about? Who at this school needs to hear the Gospel?

Gibbs: Have you ever noticed how bored and weak the student body sounds when singing hymns?

Thomasina: Yes, I have.

Gibbs: Have you ever noticed how, in class, when no one knows the answer to a theological question, someone jokingly says "Jesus," and everyone laughs? Have you ever noticed how deeply enslaved to secular culture most of the students at this school are?

Thomasina: I have.

Gibbs: That kind of enslavement is deeply demoralizing and confusing to all students, but especially students with weak faith. It drives them to believe that no one really takes Christianity seriously, that Christianity is a lost cause, that Christianity will die on their watch, and it breeds a deep skepticism toward everything their teachers and their churches claim to stand for. I wish that students at this school would labor to help other Christians retain their faith and not pretend as though they are competent to preach the

Gospel—a Gospel they rarely read, hardly understand, and about which they cannot answer basic questions.

Thomasina: So, what would you have me do?

Gibbs: Stay at this school. Cheerfully obey the rules. Do not turn a blind eye when your friends break the rules. When the occasion presents itself, sing hymns loudly. Be the kind of person that inspires others with confidence in the Christian future. Be the kind of Christian that gives others pause about believing the lie that all Christians are judgmental and self-righteous. If you cannot do it for others, do it for me, because when I hear you all blandly, indifferently sing hymns in the morning, and then go off to class excitedly talking about the perverse songs and celebrities you absolutely adore, I have to wonder whether Christianity has a future in this nation, as well. Stay at this school for another year. Stay for me and my weak faith. Sing my weak faith back to life.

DIALOGUE 8

On Dating in High School

James: What do you think about students dating in high school?

Gibbs: Why date? Why not just get married?

James: We're obviously not old enough to get married.

Gibbs: So why date?

James: I want to marry someone that I really connect with, so— look, let me lay my cards out. I am dating someone right now, but we are not dating just for fun. We really want to get to know each other better.

Gibbs: No. You are not currently in a relationship with a girl to "get to know her better," and we both know it.

James: What makes you say that?

Gibbs: I used that same pious-sounding excuse when I was your age, and my parents didn't know how to respond to it either.

James: Go on.

Gibbs: What is the purpose of "getting to know her better"?

James: To see if we are compatible.

Gibbs: Compatible for what?

James: Marriage.

Gibbs: You're not compatible for marriage. You already know that.

James: Why?

Gibbs: Because at sixteen, you're not ready to marry anyone at all, which means you can't be compatible for marriage with anyone in particular.

James: Why not?

Gibbs: It is a bit like trying to find a variety of cheese which suits the taste of someone who is allergic to milk. You don't see a problem with dating in high school, but what about elementary school? Are you in favor of students dating in elementary school?

James: No, but that is different.

ON DATING IN HIGH SCHOOL

Gibbs: How is dating in fourth grade different than dating in tenth grade?

James: Seriously? In fourth grade, you haven't even gone through puberty yet.

Gibbs: Good. That is one difference. Keep going.

James: I could think of other ways.

Gibbs: When you think of them, let me know. While I am waiting, let me give you some ways in which fourth graders and sophomores are not different. Neither is physically fully grown, neither is legally responsible for their own actions, neither pay for their own food or clothes or rent, neither have careers, neither has a high school diploma, neither is legally old enough to marry, neither can vote, neither can buy wine, neither can be drafted for war, neither has credit, neither can rent an apartment . . . I could keep going.

James: That's kind of insulting.

Gibbs: No, I would say it's just not particularly flattering. Any other ways fourth graders and sophomores are different?

James: Wouldn't you say that a sophomore has a sense of self-awareness that a fourth grader doesn't have?

Gibbs: Sometimes, but not always. A great many fourth graders are more obedient and respectful of authorities than sophomores, and I would say those are more important factors in determining readiness for marriage than mere self-awareness. The biggest difference between fourth graders and sophomores, at least so far as this conversation goes, is that sophomores want to date, but fourth graders don't.

James: You didn't answer my question, though. I want to get to know my girlfriend better to see if we are compatible as husband and wife.

Gibbs: For the sake of argument, imagine two fourth graders want to go on a date.

James: Like I said, that's different. They're not ready.

Gibbs: Let's say the fourth graders know they are not ready to get married but want to get to know each other better. How long do you suppose they would have to date before they knew they were compatible as spouses?

James: A long time.

Gibbs: How long?

James: A really long time.

Gibbs: Why?

James: They're both still changing.

Gibbs: How old should you be before you get married?

ON DATING IN HIGH SCHOOL

James: I mean, at least twenty-three or twenty-four.

Gibbs: Fourth grade is only six years behind you. Twenty-three is seven years ahead of you. Would you want the nine-year-old version of yourself choosing the girl you would date now?

James: I guess not.

Gibbs: Then why do you think the twenty-three-year-old you wants the sixteen-year-old you choosing a spouse for him?

James: It seems different, I guess.

Gibbs: If no one is ready to get married at the age of sixteen, then "getting to know" someone romantically in high school will simply terminate the relationship.

James: Why?

Gibbs: Because you will both learn the person you are dating is not yet marriage-material. I don't mean that as an insult. At sixteen, a person might have a lot of potential, but you should marry someone based on what they have done, not what you hope they will do someday. At sixteen, you just haven't accomplished enough to be worthy of marriage.

James: "Worthy of marriage"?

Gibbs: Yes. Marriage is a high and noble calling that you have to prepare for—that you have to prove yourself worthy of undertaking.

James: I might be willing to agree with that, but I still don't know why you can't accept the idea that dating couples are getting to know each other better.

Gibbs: I never said they weren't getting to know each other better, just that knowing each other better is an accident of romance, not the purpose of it.

James: What's the purpose, then?

Gibbs: What kinds of things do you like to do with your girlfriend?

James: Talk, go to the movies, text, listen to music, hang out.

Gibbs: Do you do all those things with your male friends, as well?

James: Yes.

Gibbs: But you have never told anyone that you were going to see the new *Terminator* movie with Jackson and Lucas "so you could get to know them better."

James: Going to the movies is fun. It feels good to hang out with friends. Besides, friends have to do something.

Gibbs: Agreed, and the same is true of a girlfriend. It feels good to have a girlfriend and to be around your girlfriend. This is only right, though. A friendship should exist for the sake of enjoying another person. When our friends have ulterior motives for friendship, we feel betrayed and used. Because of this, I don't buy the studious-sounding claim that a high school dating relationship is some kind of investigation, some kind of fact-finding mission wherein an extensive study is being conducted to determine the viability of a marriage. You both know that people change a lot in the first few years after high school. I am sure you are curious what the profound freedom, autonomy, and anonymity which comes with leaving home and going off to college will do to your girlfriend. She ought to be similarly curious about you.

James: What if we go to college together?

Gibbs: In order to go to the same college together, you will have to begin preparing to go to the same college together at the beginning of senior year. This means you will both have to make a monumental economic and geographical commitment to one another while still "getting to know one another." That kind of thing makes the relationship incredibly top-heavy. It means that you are asking the other person to undertake marriage-level commitments to you, but without marriage-level rights or marriage-level oaths to govern your conduct toward one another. Very few relationships survive that kind of strain.

James: So, if dating in high school is such a bad idea, I guess you have a pretty low opinion of people who do it.

Gibbs: No, that is not true. It tends to be the more responsible, more diligent students who date in high school. Dating tends to require a little ambition and given that ennui and sloth are besetting sins of this age, I have a hard time heavily faulting a student who is striving and reaching, even if I believe they are reaching too far.

James: So, if I'm not dating, what should I do if I want to prepare for marriage?

Gibbs: Do your own laundry. Get a lousy job bagging groceries as soon as you can. Poke your head in the principal's office once a week and say, "I have ten minutes and nothing to do. Do you need some chairs or tables moved around or something?" Don't get a phone. You'll have to get one when you're an adult but hold off as long as you can. Learn to cook something basic, hearty, and tasty, so you can give your mother the night off every now and again. Do pointless tasks with your dad. He probably drives to the city dump once a week or something like that. Go with him. It doesn't matter if you say anything. It's enough to be there with him. He will say something. Learn one book of the Bible really well, probably Ecclesiastes or Proverbs or St. Matthew's Gospel. When you watch movies, watch black-and-white movies. Learn a few old prayers by heart which you can say while you walk from one class to another.

James: Did you do those things to get ready for marriage?

Gibbs: Only two or three of them. The rest of them are things I do that keep me married, and so I assume they would be good in preparing for marriage, as well.

James: I'm not breaking up with my girlfriend.

Gibbs: I understand. I never broke up with any of my girlfriends and I still wear that fact as a merit badge.

James: But you don't think my relationship will work out?

ON DATING IN HIGH SCHOOL

Gibbs: No.

James: Why?

Gibbs: All the standard reasons. Sooner or later, one of the two people in the relationship realizes that marriage is not a possibility and then the whole thing begins to seem rather pointless. At the beginning of the relationship, both people are still too thrilled by the honor of having their existence affirmed by a member of the opposite sex to think about how profoundly tenuous the whole thing is.

James: But what if the point of the relationship is to glorify God?

Gibbs: When you are sixteen, you can honor God just as much in a friendship as you can in a romance.

James: But the relationship I am in now has been so good for me.

Gibbs: I can believe that. Like I said, I am not strongly opposed to high school romances. Only a little. Romantic relationships often bring out what is best in young men. A high school sophomore with a girlfriend takes better care of his appearance. He spends money on someone other than himself. He even prays more and reads his Bible more. He has a sense of duty and obligation.

James: Then why are you opposed to student relationships?

Gibbs: Because all that is merely the silver lining, and the silver lining does not last as long as the misery and confusion which results from a failed romance. Granted, a little misery is not the end of the world, and a young man learns a lot about the nature of the soul while tending to a broken heart. However, I think that most high school romances are based on faulty conceptions of romance and are generally evidence of a dangerous lack of self-awareness.

James: But not every high school relationship is doomed to fail, right? Look, I know how it sounds, but what if mine is one of the rare ones which leads all the way to marriage?

Gibbs: That is the dangerous lack of self-awareness I just referred to. Some people who date in high school end up marrying. And some arranged marriages work out happily, as well. Would you like your parents to arrange a wife for you?

James: No.

Gibbs: Me neither. That would be terribly strange, though I am sure it works out nicely every blue moon. You see, wisdom is really not concerned with outside possibilities, outliers, and unusual cases. Wisdom is concerned with human nature. Wisdom is concerned with what is normal, what is typical, and what usually happens. Being wise means not making exceptions for yourself or treating yourself as a special case. Wisdom means regarding yourself as common, average, the kind of person for whom proverbs, maxims, warning labels, cautionary tales, and generalities are applicable.

James: So, what does that have to do with dating in high school?

Gibbs: The kind of fellow who says, "I know pretty much all high school romances fail, but mine is going to last," is already thinking of himself as someone for whom conventional wisdom does not apply. I don't have a lot of confidence in someone who thinks of himself as beyond the authority of conventional wisdom. No young man who thinks himself special ought to be dating. God knows what he will justify doing on the grounds that he is special.

James: But what if I am trying to be wise in the way I date?

Gibbs: There are better and worse ways to go about nearly anything. Given that you're a pretty responsible young man, I am quite sure you're doing this ill-advised thing in a decent, orderly way. There are also more and less safe positions to take in a speeding car about to hit a brick wall.

James: Very funny. Let me ask you one more thing—and I should repeat that I am not breaking up with her—but if God didn't want teenagers involved in romances, then why does He inspire romantic feelings in teenage hearts?

Gibbs: A fine question. While God awakens the heart and the body to the desire for romantic love, wisdom demands learning to control those feelings, not be controlled by them. Man is made of the earth, and the earth must be subdued. A great many desires are natural, but we may not indulge them whenever and however we want. The desire for love emerges many years before it can reasonably or legally be satisfied. The self-control learned in those intervening years is, perhaps, the greatest preparation for marriage you can undertake. You might say that God inspires the desire for romantic love way too early so you can develop the necessary patience for marriage. Men who get married and then fall in love with someone from the office generally claim they could not help themselves—which is true, but only because they never learned self-control.

James: Are you saying that everyone out there who married after dating in high school is secretly miserable?

Gibbs: Absolutely not. I will gladly admit there are a few counterexamples to nearly everything I have said.

James: It does not bother you in the slightest that your ideas are not absolutely, universally true?

Gibbs: No. They are normally true, and I am a normal person, which makes such ideas very helpful for me. I have regular problems for which there are regular solutions.

James: What if I'm not a normal person? What if mine is a special case?

Gibbs: It might be. It just might be. I only have conversations like this one with students a dozen times a year.

DIALOGUE 9

On Optimism & Identity

Gibbs: We haven't spoken in a while. How is the school year going for you?

Carson: I won't lie. It's been a tough year.

Gibbs: How so?

Carson: Heather and I broke up last month. I just found out I need two more operations on my knee which means basketball isn't going to be a possibility next year, either. My relationship with my parents isn't great at the moment either.

Gibbs: I am sorry to hear that.

Carson: That's okay. Things will get better, right?

Gibbs: They might.

Carson: That's not very encouraging.

Gibbs: If you live long enough, things will probably get better, at least for a little while.

Carson: You wouldn't call yourself an optimist, would you?

Gibbs: What makes you say that?

Carson: Optimists believe things will get better. Haven't you seen that billboard? It shows a man crawling out of a dark tunnel into the light of day and says, "Things will get better. Optimism. Pass it on." I think that is a good message. It's positive, it's encouraging. It's what I need to keep telling myself in times like these.

Gibbs: When did you first see this billboard?

Carson: Maybe three or four months ago.

Gibbs: You saw a billboard that said, "Things will get better," and then Heather broke up with you and you found out that a series of knee surgeries would keep you from playing basketball? It seems like the billboard got it wrong.

Carson: Is it possible the billboard was referring to what would happen after Heather broke up with me?

Gibbs: That is where you are right now. This is the period after she broke up with you.

ON OPTIMISM & IDENTITY

Carson: I meant whatever comes after the period I am in now.

Gibbs: Who can say what will happen next?

Carson: An optimist believes things will get better.

Gibbs: Get better when?

Carson: At some point.

Gibbs: And that you will live long enough to see things get better?

Carson: I hope so, yes. It's not a certainty but a belief.

Gibbs: For as long as I can remember, optimism meant seeing the glass as half full, not half empty.

Carson: That strikes me as very optimistic, too.

Gibbs: But seeing the glass as half full, not half empty, requires something entirely different of a man than believing things will get better.

Carson: Aren't both sentiments born of the same hopeful spirit?

Gibbs: No. When you see the glass as half full, you see it as half full right now. It is a way of looking at the world today and being grateful for what you have today. "The glass is half full, not half empty" is a philosophical claim, a way of interpreting the gifts of God. "Things will get better" is not concerned with giving thanks for anything today. It is a way of deferring the need for gratitude until tomorrow.

Carson: You really think my life might just keep getting worse until I die?

Gibbs: It depends on what you mean by "worse."

Carson: "Worse" would mean my relationship with my father deteriorated further, as did my health, as did my relationship with my mother. And Heather never speaks to me again.

Gibbs: Is it possible those things will happen? Sure. Especially if you die next week. I don't think that will happen, though. I think your life will probably unfold in a normal manner.

Carson: What do you mean by "normal"?

Gibbs: You'll live another sixty years or so and that during that time things will get better, then they will get worse, then they will get better again, over and over again.

Carson: So, the billboard was right?

Gibbs: The claim "Things will get better" assumes "things" are in what state now?

Carson: It assumes "things" aren't all that great.

Gibbs: And yet, you live in the future that you were looking forward to five years ago, when you were twelve and could not wait to be old enough to drive, to date, to have a job and make your own money, to play varsity. You live in the "brighter" future the billboard prophesied months ago. This, at the very least, is what the glass-half-full approach would have you consider. The man who believes "Things will get better" never finds the glass half full, though, because he is constantly looking forward to the day when the glass will be entirely full.

Carson: What if the man who believes things will get better has an empty glass and he is looking forward to it being half full?

Gibbs: The half full scenario is less concerned with what a man has than what he does with what he has. It assumes everybody has something good and whether you enjoy your good things is entirely up to you. "Things will get better," and when they do, a man may still be discontent and insist things need to get even better before he can be happy.

Carson: But you do believe that things will probably get better for me?

Gibbs: Yes, I believe Fortune's wheel is always turning. "Things" are constantly changing. That is the nature of life on Earth. Money comes and goes. Fame comes and goes. Health, popularity, and power come and go and come again. In Ecclesiastes, Solomon says, "When times are good, be happy; but when times are bad, consider this: God has made the one as well as the other. Therefore, no one can discover anything about their future." (Ecclesiastes 7:14 NIV). When good times come, bless God. When bad times come, bless God. Perhaps times are bad now. If so, God has appointed these times for you and when God gives you anything, your response begins with thanks, even if you go on to complain and ask Him to change things.

Carson: Thank Him and then complain?

Gibbs: Thanking Him first is the only way your complaints will make any sense. Why ask Him to change things if He does not know what is best for you? How do you prove yourself worthy of the change you are asking for except by giving thanks first? You must first show God you understand the nature of things—that all things come from His hand—before there is any point in asking Him to change things. If you don't understand the nature of things, He might change things for you, and yet you wouldn't even know it.

Carson: Giving thanks to God for bad times strikes me as a very difficult thing to do honestly.

Gibbs: Thanking God for pain and suffering is quite difficult, and yet "Things will get better" strikes me as the sort of modern slogan which is popular because it goes down easy. It asks absolutely nothing of us. Granted, the future is ultimately unknowable, but there is a logic at work in nature—mother nature and human nature—which allows us to say how things tend to work. Suppose you saw a billboard that said, "You will lose weight. Optimism. Pass it on." How would you respond to that?

Carson: It seems a little risky to simply tell everyone in the whole world they will lose weight.

Gibbs: Does it not seem far safer to say, "You will lose weight if you diet and exercise"?

Carson: Sure.

Gibbs: And if you saw a sign that said, "You will make money. Optimism. Pass it on"?

Carson: Again, "You will make money if you go to work."

Gibbs: Agreed. While there is no guarantee that diet and exercise will bring weight loss, diet and exercise have a well-documented history of bringing weight loss, just like an industrious spirit coupled with hard work has a well-documented history of bringing income. However, telling perfect strangers that things will unconditionally get better is setting them up for failure. If a man believed he would unconditionally lose weight over the coming year, why not eagerly anticipate that weight loss from the comfort of his sofa with a fat slice of chocolate cake?

Carson: So why did the optimistic billboard not provide a few suggestions on how people could usher in this brighter future?

Gibbs: Real optimism is good and valuable. Every good and valuable thing in the world inspires a market for fakes.

Carson: You think "Things will get better" is fake optimism?

Gibbs: Absolutely. Glass-half-full optimism requires people to give thanks for the good things in their lives and to make the most of those things, not simply wait around for better things to come.

Believing things will necessarily get better, though—regardless of what we think or do or say—is one aspect of the fake optimism which is fashionable in our day. Another aspect is giving thanks for whatever things we have, whether they are good or not.

Carson: Should we not rejoice in all things?

Gibbs: Should an alcoholic rejoice that he is an alcoholic?

Carson: No.

Gibbs: An alcoholic could rejoice that he finally had the courage, humility, and clarity of thought to admit he was an alcoholic, though. He could rejoice that he finally knew he had to change his ways.

Carson: Of course.

Gibbs: I know you are too old for bedtime stories, but it would serve you well to thumb through a few popular children's books the next time you are in a Barnes & Noble. There is no better place to view fake optimism than in the drivel adults now force on unsuspecting elementary school students. The modern children's book is uncomfortably stuffed full of good feelings and curiously free of any real drama.

Carson: This cannot strike you as a new phenomenon. The drama in children's books is usually pretty low stakes, right?

Gibbs: Low stakes, not no stakes. Until about twenty years ago, children's books were almost all about some little child overcoming a common problem, like a dying pet, a school bully, a fear of crowds. The average child in a children's book began the story as a picky eater and finished the story asking for more veal cutlets. In the middle, the parent reading the story learned a lesson about how to help their child overcome the problem. Very few popular children's books tell such stories these days, though. The plot of the modern children's book is, "Let's celebrate fifty things Brooklyn can be when she grows up." Brooklyn doesn't actually do anything in the book, though. She doesn't overcome shyness, fear, or cowardice. Brooklyn isn't praised for what she has accomplished, but for what she is, regardless of what she is. That's the fake version of "rejoicing in all things."

Carson: I see. You can't help a child overcome a problem unless you first admit the child has a problem.

Gibbs: And the modern man is terrified of suggesting a child has a problem. Hence, the problem is not really that a certain child is fat, but that the child thinks being fat is a problem. Celebrating different body shapes and sizes is the way to overcome overeating.

Carson: As opposed to eating less.

Gibbs: Right. The problem is not that some children watch too much television. The problem is that watching too much television has been stigmatized. The solution is celebrating the fact that some children enjoy television, and some children enjoy playing outside. This way, no one has to change. The problem is not that some people live pointless and perverse lives. The problem is that they are deeply depressed about it. The solution is to give them drugs that take away the depression they feel about their pointless, perverse lives.

Carson: That way, they don't have to change.

Gibbs: Telling anyone they ought to do anything is cruel, intrusive, and shows a lack of empathy.

Carson: So, what does real optimism ask people to see which fake optimism does not?

Gibbs: The half full approach acknowledges the glass is only half full, not entirely full, and that the glass may never be entirely full. The half full approach is not a denial that things could always be better, but it is an assertion that any man who takes an honest assessment of his life will find he truly has some abilities, some gifts, and some resources, even if others have more. Fake optimism robs a man of his abilities and gifts because it teaches him that his abilities aren't worth more than his disabilities. When a fellow equates his disabilities with his abilities, he doesn't end up with twice as much as he had before. He ends up with nothing.

Carson: At times, it can be very hard to see those gifts and abilities, though.

Gibbs: Especially if no one has the courage to tell you that you're obligated to see them.

Carson: So, now that I am armed with real optimism, am I bound to get ahead in the world?

Gibbs: Get ahead of who?

ON OPTIMISM & IDENTITY

Carson: The people with fake optimism.

Gibbs: I couldn't say. The modern world is slanted toward those with fake optimism. Real optimism is thought exploitative.

Carson: Why?

Gibbs: People who acknowledge that they have gifts, abilities, and resources are regarded as thieves and hoarders.

Carson: What about the man who is content with having very few gifts and abilities?

Gibbs: That man is typically judged to be delusional. Those with great gifts and abilities have tricked him into submission and conned him into giving up his complaint.

Carson: So, I can either embrace fake optimism, in which case I simply wait around for a goodness that never arrives, or I can embrace real optimism, struggle for goodness, and be accused of thieving and hoarding by people who refuse to lift a finger.

Gibbs: It might even be worse than that, though, because fakery is parasitic and feeds on reality. Forged currency can be spent only because real currency exists, although forged currency drives down the value of real currency.

Carson: Are so many people really content to sit around doing nothing, though?

Gibbs: There is a considerable difference between not doing anything and not doing anything profitable. We are living through the age of professional video gamers, after all. A blithe insistence that things will get better is based on a view of man which is basically devoid of moral agency.

Carson: What does that mean?

Gibbs: The modern man prefers an amoral conception of his own identity, a conception that coincides with the idea that no one should be told to do anything difficult.

Carson: How can an identity hold moral weight? Isn't it good to be Joshua Gibbs only if Joshua Gibbs is good?

Gibbs: Joshua Gibbs is the convergence of a great number of identities and loyalties. Joshua Gibbs is an Orthodox Christian, a member of St. Cyprian of Carthage Orthodox Church, a man, an American, a father, a son, a husband, a teacher, and twenty other things of varying degrees of importance. Each of those identities and loyalties requires something of me. There are good men and bad men. Good Americans and bad Americans. Good teachers and bad teachers. All of the identities and loyalties I profess are also standards that I can be held to. Being a husband means I must do certain things and must not do other things. If I do what I must, I am a good husband. If not, I am a bad husband. The same is true of being an American, an Orthodox Christian, and so forth.

Carson: What sort of identity does not hold a moral weight?

ON OPTIMISM & IDENTITY

Gibbs: The sorts of identities offered by psychologists and personality tests.

Carson: Why don't those identities have a moral weight?

Gibbs: The fact a certain man is a Christian means he cannot go to strip clubs, cannot get drunk, cannot skip church simply because he feels like it. However, the modern man is bored by the identity offered by his church. He is far more taken with the fact that he is INTJ, or a Type Two on the Enneagram, or an introvert, or an empath, none of which require him to do anything.

Carson: You mean there is no such thing as a bad introvert?

Gibbs: Yes. Bad introverts are just extroverts. Bad INTJs are just ESFPs. If you see one of your Christian friends about to enter a strip club, you can yell, "Hey, Bill, you can't go in there. You're a Christian." But if the same fellow shows up at your New Year's Eve party, you can't say, "Go home, Bill, you're an introvert." Claiming to be an introvert doesn't oblige you to stay at home on a Friday night. Similarly, INTJs are under no obligation to stay INTJs. The modern man prefers identities that are endlessly changeable and alterable. The very idea of loyalty sends the modern man into anaphylactic shock.

Carson: That's true of Christians, as well.

Gibbs: How so?

Carson: When Christians introduce themselves to non-Christians, they often begin by throwing other Christians under the bus. They say, "I'm a Christian, but I'm not one of those Christians who…"

Gibbs: I regularly hear that sort of thing, as well. When Christians introduce themselves to one another, they often do the same thing, but with their churches. They say, "I go to First Presbyterian, but I'm not really into the music." We want people to know that our churches are lucky to have us, not the other way around. The modern man obeys no one but his own conscience. Loyalty is for suckers.

Carson: If being a Type Two or an INTJ doesn't carry any moral weight, why are so many people enthralled by personality tests?

Gibbs: Personality tests offer the illusion of self-knowledge with very little work. Up until the twentieth century, Christians believed that self-knowledge came only by way of humility, prayer, and repentance. Self-knowledge was the fruit of a lifetime of intellectual labor and struggle. "Know thyself" was the command which typified philosophy, man's timeless search for wisdom. Today, we believe self-knowledge can be acquired in about twenty minutes by answering a brief questionnaire that poses questions like, "How deeply do you feel your emotions?" and "How much do you enjoy going to art museums?"

Carson: But I have taken personality tests before and found them helpful.

Gibbs: What would you say to a person who claimed to find horoscopes helpful?
Carson: I would want to know how horoscopes were helpful.

Gibbs: How was the personality test helpful?

Carson: The test told me about myself.

Gibbs: Did you, by any chance, tell the test quite a bit about yourself first?

Carson: I suppose so.

Gibbs: So you answered some questions about yourself and then some algorithm told you that you have quite a lot in common with Stephen Hawking, Winston Churchill, and Rosa Parks?

Carson: You make it sound so tawdry, but the whole thing made me feel quite special.

Gibbs: Of course it did. "Things will get better" also makes people feel special. It makes them believe they live in a momentous age, an age which is about to give birth to something sublime and eternal. People also enjoy feeling they will play an important role in bringing about this sublime, eternal thing—and yet, they tend to simultaneously believe they will bring this thing about without effort or sacrifice, simply by being themselves.

Carson: What if it is good to think of yourself as having something in common with Winston Churchill?

Gibbs: You do not need an internet algorithm to tell you that you have something in common with Winston Churchill. Obviously, you do. You're both men. You're both Christians. You're both Anglicans. There is at least one significant difference between you, though.

Carson: What is that?

Gibbs: Churchill accomplished many great things. You have not accomplished many great things yet, which means you must be careful not to flatter yourself by comparing yourself with him. If you want to be like Churchill, you cannot simply be yourself. You must do great things, as well. However, you can imitate the virtue of any righteous man or woman. You don't need some algorithm on the internet to give you permission to imitate the wisdom and wit of Winston Churchill.

Carson: I understand that, but I remember clearly the first time I took a personality test. It felt so good to have someone tell me, "This is who you are. There is a name—a title—for what you are. This is what you can do. These are some great people like you." I thought about it constantly in the days which followed. I found myself sitting up straighter in class. Paying attention. Saying more clever things. I wanted to keep the feeling, but it wouldn't last.

Gibbs: That fact it did not last might have something to do with the fact that the test did not have any real authority over you. At best, those tests typically make a few grammatical and aesthetic nods to "science," as though they have something in common with molecular biology or nuclear physics.

Carson: Is there nothing scientific about them?
Gibbs: If personality tests are scientific, they cannot carry moral

weight. Science speaks to what is, not what ought to be. Science cannot tell us what is morally right because morality is a spiritual and ontological concern, both of which are beyond the reach of science. Morality is the province of philosophy and theology. If personality tests are philosophical, though, the fact they are so new makes them highly suspect because it means they are not part of the tradition of Plato, Augustine, Aquinas, Calvin, and so forth. They are part of some novel, unproven philosophy that must prove its worth; however, if personality tests were truthful and accurate, I would expect there to have been some watershed cultural change in this country around the time they became popular. There is no dispute today about whether penicillin works. The proof is that almost no one dies of scarlet fever anymore. Personality tests, on the other hand, have made identity so radically unstable, that many people no longer believe identity even exists—at least not in the way people believed identity existed in bygone centuries.

Carson: I would say that identity matters more now than in the past. People argue about it constantly.

Gibbs: These days, what is regarded as the most important aspect of a person's identity?

Carson: Their gender. Or their race, perhaps. It regularly changes depending on the news cycle.

Gibbs: Consider the person who designed the "Things will get better" billboard. If that person were being interviewed on CNN and was asked what it meant to be a man, what do you suppose he would say?
Carson: I imagine he would get very uncomfortable.

Gibbs: I would be uncomfortable, too.

Carson: I think he would say that everybody gets to determine for himself what it means to be a man.

Gibbs: And if we all get to determine for ourselves what it means to be a man, is there such a thing as a fake man?

Carson: No, I suppose not.

Gibbs: And if there is no such thing as a fake man, is there such a thing as a real man?

Carson: I see your point. If there is no standard by which a person is judged a man, then the concept of "man" more or less drifts off into space.

Gibbs: If there is no standard for a man, then the world does not need men. Standards are predicated on the concept of purpose, and if there are no standards which make a certain person a man, then a man simply cannot and does not do anything. The same is true of any identity, though. And yet, your story about briefly taking inspiration from the claim you had something in common with Churchill rings true—sadly true.

Carson: Did you go through something similar?

Gibbs: I have cycled through many different identities in the last twenty-five years, yes.

ON OPTIMISM & IDENTITY

Carson: Did you settle on one?

Gibbs: Yes, but not until after I married and had children. I could have settled on a particular identity well before that point, but I was too arrogant.

Carson: What does arrogance have to do with it?

Gibbs: We change our identities to hide. We are ashamed of who or what we are—not necessarily because we have done something wicked, but because we are shallow and petty. This, at least, is the explanation Walker Percy offers in *Lost in the Cosmos*. Percy says we endlessly alter our identities because we are afraid of being recognized. When a man is recognized, he can be held accountable for his actions.

Carson: What sort of identities did you adopt?

Gibbs: It began when I was around twelve or thirteen, which is when it begins for most people. That is the age at which your body begins to transform, which is unsettling and confusing. All sorts of new desires and thoughts plague you, most of which you keep secret from your parents. This is the age when you reject the clothes your parents have given you. You want to dress yourself, and clothing is one of the most important aspects of carving out an identity for yourself. "The clothes make the man," as they say.

Carson: I remember the first time I picked out my own clothes. It was the summer before seventh grade.

Gibbs: This is also the point at which you begin spending more time by yourself, unsupervised. Adolescence is really a return to the Garden of Eden—to the Fall, that is.

Carson: How so?

Gibbs: When Adam sinned, he quit thinking of God and God's gifts and thought only of himself and what he wanted, what could benefit him, and what suited his tastes. It was this self-awareness and self-centeredness that opened their eyes to their nakedness. They rejected the clothing God had given them, made clothes for themselves, then hid from God.

Carson: What clothing had God given them?

Gibbs: They were "clothed in modesty," as many great theologians have said.

Carson: I never thought of their hiding as a desire to be alone, but I see the point. I didn't want to be alone—away from my parents, I mean—until I had something to hide.

Gibbs: Whether or not you buy the idea they were "clothed in modesty," it is nonetheless true Adam and Eve wanted to dress themselves. It is impossible to say whether they did so purposefully, although it must be noted they dressed themselves in a way God did not approve. You may recall God refused to allow them to leave the Garden dressed in fig leaves. He made them clothes of animal skins. Likewise, many of the clothes teenagers choose for themselves rile and vex their parents, even if just a little. Very few people move from the somewhat shapeless, asexual clothes given to children directly into the modest yuppie workwear sold by J. Crew. There is often something intentionally provocative about the way adolescents dress themselves.

Carson: I think the first article of clothing I desperately wanted was a band T-shirt.

Gibbs: And the band was?

Carson: Just somebody my parents hated.

Gibbs: Obviously. From the moment you choose your own clothes, you become very anxious for your friends to see you so that they understand you have changed, become self-aware, and taken possession of your own soul. If the clothing does not vex your parents just a little, it cannot prove your independence.

Carson: And you are always quite embarrassed when anyone comments that you "look different." You want people to notice you look different, but not to point it out. When someone points it out, it only confirms they still remember you from when you were young and naive.

Gibbs: From the point I began choosing my own clothes, I moved from one self to another rather frequently for the next twelve years. But it is not enough to merely change one's uniform. A whole new set of manners, music, books, and habits are necessary, as well.
Carson: Is that sort of thing not natural to adolescence, though?

Gibbs: The attempt to find "the real you" through trial and error?

Carson: Yes.

Gibbs: Some people settle rather quickly into an image they retain for many years. I suppose someone might discover punk music at fifteen and commit the following twenty years to the punk ethos.

Carson: Don't you think there is something admirable about that?

Gibbs: I do. However, most of the personalities we try on during adolescence—punk, nerd, preppie, queer, jock—cannot be sustained for an entire lifetime, at least not by people who want to experience all that adulthood has to offer.

Carson: Why not?

Gibbs: Because everyone smirks at the oldest man in the club—and he knows it. The oldest man in the club failed to grow up, which means it is hard to trust him with adult responsibilities. His desires and interests are stuck back in a stage of life where very little was required of him. It is easy to spot someone who never gave up the freedom and glory of youth.

Carson: So, switching from one self to another is a dead end, but so is landing on a particular self during adolescence and never letting go of it?

Gibbs: The problem with constantly switching from one self to another is not that it is a dead end, but that it leads to a shallow conception of who you are. The only way you can regularly manipulate and edit the self is by reducing the self to something petty, paltry, and manageable, after which point you view your soul as nothing more than an avatar, a doll to be dressed up, or a pet that is photographed for the amusement of friends.

Carson: What does it mean to have a deep self, then?

Gibbs: The sorts of people who have vast, weighty souls have undertaken the Herculean labor of reconciling their lives with transcendent institutions and identities.

Carson: Like what?

Gibbs: Father, son, husband, Catholic, Presbyterian, teacher, and so forth. It matters that there are good teachers, fathers, husbands, and wives, too. Being a good father is something a man can take contentment in. A robust discussion of fatherhood will prompt a room full of men to talk about their own fathers, good fathers, the sort of fathers they ought to be. Taking a personality test allows a man to talk about himself, which makes him feel important; however, talking about fatherhood or Presbyterianism or marriage makes a man understand the burden that has been placed on his shoulders and inspires him to carry it faithfully.

Carson: So, once you decided to become a father, you quit looking for an identity?

Gibbs: Once I became a father, I realized that being a good father would be a blessing to someone other than myself. A good father produces something: happy, stable children. "Goths", "gamers", "nerds", "preppies", "queers", and so forth are not morally obligated to produce anything the world needs, which means they aren't sustainable identities.

Carson: Sustainable?

Gibbs: They're not satisfying. In our day, the less productive a certain identity is, the more people of that identity demand to be celebrated. Productive people don't demand to be celebrated, though. They don't care, and they don't have the time. A productive person claims, "Whether others celebrate me or not, I have to continue my work." On the other hand, people who cannot generate their own reasons for staying alive have to command others to generate those reasons, typically by demanding unwarranted praise. The modern man does not want praise for what he has done, but for what he is, regardless of what he is. The unwarranted praise he demands goes hand-in-hand with the unwarranted belief things will get better.

Carson: So, what should I do? I'm not a father yet.

Gibbs: You aren't too young to settle into other roles, though. Father is part of my identity, but I'm also a husband, a son, an Orthodox Christian, and a teacher. I didn't find any of those roles satisfying until quite late in life, though. From the time I was fifteen until I was nearly thirty, I prided myself on being a film junkie and a pop music aficionado, neither of which has ultimately proven to be worth all that much to me. Back then, my interest moved from one kind of film to another and one genre of rock to another, but now most of my former interests run together. Almost none of the things I was interested in could be taken into adulthood.

Carson: Why couldn't they be taken into adulthood?

Gibbs: Because the sort of people who I wanted and needed to take me seriously—not only to advance my career but to build a happy family—didn't take those youthful interests all that seriously.

Carson: Why didn't they take those interests seriously?

Gibbs: Because those interests revolved around having fun and feeling good, neither of which pay the bills or help little children cheerfully obey.

Carson: So, I need interests I can take into adulthood?

Gibbs: You need to begin committing yourself to things you can love for the rest of your life. Loving something for a long time is what keeps a man from becoming shallow.

Carson: How does it do that?

Gibbs: The longer you love something, the more you have to suffer for it. A short-lived love requires very little sacrifice. New things are exciting, funny, sexy, fashionable. None of those qualities is all that important, so we don't invest much in new things, which makes it easy to give them up when newer, more fashionable things come along. If you want to love things for a lifetime, you have to choose things with qualities that are worthy of suffering. To love a thing for a long time is to love it in good times and bad, in sickness and in health, when it is fashionable and when it is despised. To love a thing for a short time is to love what that thing can do for you. We only love things for a long time that deserve our love, though.

Carson: What deserves my love?

Gibbs: Your father and mother deserve your love, as does your God, your church, your country, and your school. The earth itself deserves your love, as do noble things, godlike things, and things of great beauty. All enduring testimonies to the truth deserve your love. If you commit your life to things which deserve your love, your suffering will point to something higher and better than yourself. Your suffering will mean something, which will make it endurable. If the only person you're willing to suffer for is yourself, suicide is a reasonable solution to any problem.

DIALOGUE 10

On Learning

Noah: I just finished reading a great book, and I thought you might like to borrow it.

Gibbs: What's the book?

Noah: It's a Marxist interpretation of Mark's Gospel.

Gibbs: I'm not interested in that sort of thing.

Noah: Really? Why not?

Gibbs: I am not a Marxist, and I do not want to become one.

Noah: You're afraid that reading a Marxist book might make you a Marxist?

Gibbs: That's how it tends to work. Did reading this book make you a Marxist?

Noah: Before I read the book, I didn't really understand Marxism. Having finished the book, I don't know if I'd call myself a full-blown Marxist, but I'm certainly more sympathetic towards Marxism.

Gibbs: And you want me to be more sympathetic toward Marxism?

Noah: I suppose so. But you're a literature teacher. I thought you people weren't afraid of books.

Gibbs: You are quite mistaken. We're more afraid of books than anyone.

Noah: But you're a teacher. You help people learn. Shouldn't people continue learning for their entire lives?

Gibbs: That depends entirely on what you mean by "learn."

Noah: You don't honestly think people reach a point where they should stop reading, do you?

Gibbs: I think people should read books until they die, but not just any books. I think the range of books people read should narrow as they grow older.

Noah: Won't that make them close-minded?

Gibbs: It will close their minds to certain beliefs, yes. If a mind isn't closed off to certain beliefs, it hasn't truly grasped anything. Grasping one belief means closing your mind off from other beliefs. That is simply how grasping works. For example, grasping an object in your hand—a pair of dice, say—means not grasping other objects. The mind works a bit differently, but the principle is the same.

Noah: How does the mind work differently?

Gibbs: The mind doesn't grasp just one thing. The mind can grasp many things. It can grasp some things tightly and some things loosely. The mind can let go of one idea while retaining others.

Noah: You're not all that old, though.

Gibbs: That's true, but I would say a healthy mind begins closing itself off to certain beliefs quite early.

Noah: When did your mind begin closing?

Gibbs: A good many of the beliefs I now have about politics, reason, religion, and aesthetics took hold around twelve years ago when I was in my late twenties. My mind began closing to certain intellectual possibilities back then. The most important beliefs I have today began to settle into my heart back then and have gradually deepened and intensified ever since.

Noah: If those beliefs are so deep and intense, why are you afraid to read a book which challenges them? Can't your belief stand up to a challenge?

Gibbs: If a certain businessman has been faithful to the same woman for twenty years, he can probably withstand the temptation of a beautiful young secretary, but he would be a fool to seek out that sort of temptation. If the temptation comes to him and he cannot avoid being tempted, that is one thing, but Christians must pray that God would not lead them into temptation.

Noah: Doesn't it seem cowardly to not read a book simply because you're afraid you would be convinced by it? Suppose some atheist refused to read a book about Christianity because he was afraid he'd be convinced it was right and have to change the way he lived?

Gibbs: If that's the only reason he won't read it, it doesn't seem cowardly. It just seems lazy.

Noah: Are there other reasons you don't want to read a book about Marxism?

Gibbs: Of course. My time could be better spent reading books by people I already respect. Roger Scruton is one of my favorite thinkers on the subject of politics, though he has a book about sex and a book about wine that I haven't read. I would rather spend my time reading those books than some book on Marxism.

Noah: Couldn't you better defend your own ideas by coming to grips with other ideas?

Gibbs: I don't have a lot of trouble defending my ideas. Between the two of us, I think you're closer to cracking than I am.

Noah: How come?
Gibbs: You're not all that committed to Marxism. You read one book you liked. You don't have much invested in it, which means you're

likely to read a different book about a different political ideology in the next year or two and leave Marxism behind.

Noah: Isn't that what it means to be a life-long learner?

Gibbs: Yes, which is why I have no interest in being a life-long learner. These days, a "life-long learner" is someone who goes with the flow. Fortune 500 companies create professional development plans for their employees and boast about how their employees are "constantly learning and growing," but that language thinly veils the fact the company gutlessly adheres to only the most fashionable ethics. A company that is "constantly learning and growing" can pat itself on the back whenever it cravenly updates its corporate values to reflect what is popular. There is absolutely nothing humble about it. "Our employees are constantly learning and growing" is code for, "We cravenly follow the crowd, regardless of where it goes."

Noah: Do you never read books outside your comfort zone?

Gibbs: My deepest convictions are not my "comfort zone." I suffer for my beliefs. My beliefs are my discomfort zone.

Noah: You know what I mean.

Gibbs: Based on the reasons you read one book about Marxism, do you have any reason to read another book about Marxism?

Noah: Of course. I find it fascinating.
Gibbs: Why read another book about Marxism when you could read a book about distributism?

Noah: Oh, what's that?

Gibbs: You're intellectually promiscuous.

Noah: I'm open-minded. I'm generous.

Gibbs: "I'll let you sleep with my wife if you let me sleep with yours" is not generosity.

Noah: Look, how do you think people become persuaded of new things? How do you think atheists become Christians?

Gibbs: You've never seen an atheist become a Christian.

Noah: So?

Gibbs: How do you think people become persuaded of new things?

Noah: The same way I became persuaded of Marxism.

Gibbs: You're not persuaded of Marxism. You're interested in it, and you think it's neat, but you haven't suffered anything for it. You haven't made a formal commitment to Marxism. You're not responsible to any Marxist authority who has the right to command your beliefs. You're free to define and redefine Marxism however you want. All of which means it is entirely unfair to compare your newfound interest in Marxism to Christian conversion.

Noah: Do you want atheists out there to read books about Christianity?

ON LEARNING

Gibbs: Yes.

Noah: Okay, then.

Gibbs: Go on. I want atheists to read Christian books; what does that prove?

Noah: It proves you should read this book about Marxism.

Gibbs: How does it prove that?

Noah: You have to be the change you want to see in the world.

Gibbs: How do you think this works? If I read your book on Marxism, atheists out there will be subtly more inclined to read books about Christianity? The more non-Christian books I read, the more Christian books atheists around the globe will read?

Noah: No, that's not how—

Gibbs: Perhaps if I read enough non-Christian books, I will give up the faith; then I can start reading Christian books again.

Noah: "Do unto others as you would have them do unto you," right? If you want other people to read your books, you have to read theirs.

Gibbs: I don't want other people to begrudgingly read my books, so I'm not willing to begrudgingly read theirs. In our day, Christians suffer from a misguided notion that unbelievers will be won over by our willingness to do whatever they ask, no matter how tasteless it is, no matter how stupid it is, and no matter how many of our own traditions we have to betray in the process. When Christians bow to the whims of unbelievers, they tell themselves they are "building bridges," which is true. The problem is that very few unbelievers use these bridges to enter the church, and droves of believers use these bridges to exit the church.

Noah: What should you do to draw people into the church then?

Gibbs: For the first several hundred years of church history, what drew people in was the willingness of Christians to be tortured for their belief in the resurrection of Jesus Christ. The church grows fastest and truest when it makes the fewest compromises. That's why, "I'll read your book if you'll read mine," doesn't really work.

Noah: Wait, why?

Gibbs: It immediately devalues the book you hand the other fellow. If you have to bribe and flatter someone to read a book, the book can't be all that good.

Noah: What do you say, then? "I'm not going to read your book, but you should read mine"?

Gibbs: If someone said that to you, wouldn't you be far more interested in the book they were offering?

Noah: It's so close-minded.

ON LEARNING

Gibbs: It would probably offend you the first time you heard it. After you thought about it awhile, though, you would probably realize that not all minds are closed for the same reason. Some minds are closed because they're broken, but some minds are closed because they have found something worth closing on, something they are afraid of losing.

Noah: How do you tell the difference?

Gibbs: If a man's mind is closed because it's broken, you can usually tell by observing his whole life. If some twenty-nine-year-old unemployed bachelor who lives in squalor and spends his welfare checks on liquor has a closed mind, it's probably broken. If a happily married father of three has a closed mind, it's probably because he wants to hold on to the good things he's got.

Noah: But there are happily married fathers of three who aren't Christians.

Gibbs: True. And provided those men stay happily married fathers of three, it is very difficult for them to hear and believe the Gospel. It often takes some sort of personal tragedy to bring such people to God. The earliest Christian missionaries found conversions were very rare in prosperous pagan cities that had booming economies.

Noah: How do you know when to close your mind on something?

Gibbs: A Christian mind should close more firmly on Christianity than anything else—and the way a Christian mind closes on Christianity should be fundamentally different than the way it closes on anything else. Scripture teaches us to honor our parents, but Scripture also teaches us that whoever is not willing to leave his family to follow Christ is no true follower. From this, we can see the importance of rightly ordering our loves, and love of God has priority over all other loves. That does not mean our other loves are arbitrary, though. I am a conservative, which entails a great many beliefs about tradition, the past, human nature, time, creation, and so forth. While none of those beliefs is salvific, God has nonetheless used those lesser beliefs in my salvation.

Noah: How?

Gibbs: My beliefs about tradition, the past, human nature, and so forth play a significant role in how I raise my daughters—what I allow them to watch, to listen to, to read. They figure into the way I explain good taste and common sense to them. When I lay awake at night and brood over the day, my beliefs about creation and tradition help me make sense of my failures and other people's failures, as well. God has commanded me to stay faithful to my wife, but my certainty that I would be miserable if I had an affair is born of conservative beliefs about human nature. At the age of forty, I have managed to create a stable family and a good career for myself, and I genuinely enjoy spending time with my wife and children. I credit this happiness to my beliefs—to living them out. My beliefs have served me well. They have kept me sane, kept me praying, kept me in church.

Noah: I can't say the same.
Gibbs: At sixteen, no one can. That is why young people alter their beliefs so easily. This is true for Christians, as well. They go to college,

meet die-hard leftist professors who aren't willing to "read yours if you read mine," and they're roundly impressed because they've never encountered that sort of faith before. It's why multitudes of young Christians quit the faith.

Noah: Did you alter your beliefs when you were young, as well?

Gibbs: Of course. I went through a period where I flirted with pacifism, universalism, Marxism, and all the rest.

Noah: How long did it last?

Gibbs: Until my first child was born.

DIALOGUE 11

On Finding Your Voice

Kelly: Why was the grade I got on this essay so low?

Gibbs: Did you read the comments? It was one of the most unusual essays I've ever received from a student.

Kelly: How so?

Gibbs: You kept switching tenses. Sometimes you wrote in first person, sometimes second person. There were a dozen sentences composed of just two words. You quoted Disney villains as though they were authoritative philosophers.

Kelly: I know. I'm trying to find my voice. I guess I need to keep looking.

Gibbs: What does it mean to "find your voice"?

Kelly: Everybody is different. Everybody has their own unique voice, but we all have to figure out what makes us different. I want to be a writer, but I can't be a great writer unless I dig.

Gibbs: Dig?

Kelly: I need to dig into my soul, sort through my soul, and find whatever it is that makes me unlike other people. Whatever that is, it is my voice. I must speak in that unique voice in order to be true and honest.

Gibbs: I see. How long does it take most writers to find their voice?

Kelly: It can take a long time. Umberto Eco didn't publish his first novel until he was forty-eight.

Gibbs: That's true. Was *The Name of the Rose* written in Eco's authentic voice?

Kelly: It was wildly popular, so he must have been doing something right.

Gibbs: And what was the "right" thing he was doing?

Kelly: Writing in his own voice.

Gibbs: And where does your voice come from?

Kelly: Your voice comes from your soul. Just as your soul is unique, so is your voice.

ON FINDING YOUR VOICE

Gibbs: People generally try to find things that are lost, though. Is your voice lost?

Kelly: I have faith it exists.

Gibbs: How do you know the lousy essay you wrote isn't actually written in your voice? Perhaps your voice just isn't any good.

Kelly: That's a rude thing to say.

Gibbs: As someone who can't carry a tune in a bucket, I come by such rudeness honestly.

Kelly: I have faith my voice is good.

Gibbs: Then what if I had told you the essay you wrote was very good?

Kelly: To be honest, I didn't think the essay was very good when I turned it in. I thought you might see something in it, though. A lot of people didn't think Jackson Pollock's art was any good, but a few critics saw something special in it. There was this small part of me which wondered if that would happen with my essay, too.

Gibbs: The fact that one teacher didn't like your essay is proof the essay wasn't written in your voice?

Kelly: I guess not, although I wasn't all that happy with it in the first place.

Gibbs: What I saw in your essay was a desperate desire to be original, although you seem to think it is allowable to sacrifice clarity, unity, and tradition in order to obtain originality—and not just allowable, but necessary.

Kelly: Isn't it?

Gibbs: Before I answer, let me point out that you sometimes speak of your voice as though it were a discrete object, a misplaced thing that needs to be located, while at other times you claim your voice is like your soul, but a soul is not a discrete object.

Kelly: It's not?

Gibbs: No. A soul isn't like a set of car keys you lose and then have to find again. A soul is a thing which expands, grows, evolves, or devolves into something righteous or wicked.

Kelly: Every soul is original, though. No two souls are alike.

Gibbs: There are no two souls that are the same, but all human souls are alike. If they weren't alike, they wouldn't all be souls.

Kelly: In what way are they all alike?

Gibbs: The conditions necessary for any human being to achieve contentment are largely the same. We all must learn not to lie, cheat, steal, and murder. Greed and envy are bad for all souls. Charity and mercy are good for all souls. Wickedness destroys a soul. Righteousness strengthens a soul.

ON FINDING YOUR VOICE

Kelly: What does that have to do with writing?

Gibbs: At the moment, nothing. But it has quite a bit to do with originality.

Kelly: How so?

Gibbs: If lying, cheating, stealing, and murdering are bad for every soul, then we have to admit that originality doesn't have much to offer morality.

Kelly: What does that mean?

Gibbs: It means someone who takes an original approach to the ethics of murder isn't a hero, but a villain. If some fellow running for mayor promised to take "a wildly innovative approach to the morality of rape and kidnapping," no sane person would vote for him. Sane people believe that rape and kidnapping are wrong—not just wrong for some people, but for everybody, in every era of human history.

Kelly: Fine, but isn't art a bit different from morality?

Gibbs: Perhaps, but I'd like to hear you explain why.

Kelly: Art is a matter of self-expression.

Gibbs: Morality is a matter of self-expression, as well. If you give ten dollars to a beggar, that's self-expression. If you steal ten dollars from a beggar, that's also self-expression.

A PARLEY WITH YOUTH

Kelly: Stealing from a beggar may be self-expression, but it's also wrong.

Gibbs: Agreed. The fact that something is self-expression doesn't mean it is without moral content.

Kelly: You think some art is wicked?

Gibbs: Yes, and I also believe some art is profoundly righteous.

Kelly: I know you, though. I know the kind of books you read and the kind of art you like. You can't tell me that originality doesn't matter at all. You like El Greco. You like Dante. Before Dante wrote it, there was never a poem like *The Divine Comedy,* and there hasn't been one since. It's wildly original.

Gibbs: That's sort of true, but your understanding of how Dante came up with something original is all wrong.

Kelly: I think I know what the word "original" means.

Gibbs: The last essay you wrote for me—the one we both believe is no good—was quite original. I've never read anything quite like it. It was a wholly unique assemblage of bad ideas and bad impulses.

Kelly: Don't you find completely derivative art pointless and dull, though?

Gibbs: Most derivative art is dull because it aims to be wildly original. The sort of people who make originality a top priority are dull because they draw from a laughably small pool of influences. These days, every "wildly original" artist is either imitating de Sade or Duchamp: full-blown hedonism or full-blown Gnosticism. The less interested in originality you are, the more wide and diverse your influences can become. The artist who doesn't care about being unique can draw from Michelangelo, Joyce, Bach, and Ingmar Bergman at the same time and not lose any sleep. And what a cadre of masters that would be!

Kelly: Is that what you think originality means?

Gibbs: Inasmuch as originality is a desirable quality, yes. That's simply how good original work happens.

Kelly: Explain.

Gibbs: When you sat down to write your essay, you weren't trying to create something good, so you didn't. A knowledge of good writing didn't mysteriously arrive in your head through dreams or inspirations. You know what good writing is because you've read good writing. You've read Joyce. You've read Nabokov. You've read St. Paul's epistle to the Hebrews. Who was the writer that made you want to be a writer?

Kelly: Mary Shelley. I wanted to be a writer ever since we read *Frankenstein* freshman year.

Gibbs: And what was the first thing you wrote after *Frankenstein* made you want to become a writer?

Kelly: A twenty-page long knock-off of *Frankenstein*.

Gibbs: Tell me about it.

Kelly: It was this story about a kid who wishes he had a brother, then discovers he actually has a brother, so he tracks him down, finally decides he hates his brother, and tries to kill him.

Gibbs: Sounds like a decent plot to me. What did you call the story?

Kelly: "Brothers."

Gibbs: When you sat down to write "Brothers," who were you trying to please?

Kelly: I know this sounds strange, but—

Gibbs: You were trying to please Mary Shelley?

Kelly: Yes. How did you know?

Gibbs: Because Elmore Leonard was the writer who made me want to be a writer and the first dozen stories I wrote were all intended to impress him, even though I knew he'd never read them. That's intuition. That's love, which is the only genuinely creative impulse there is. Everything other than love is just dressed-up destruction.

Kelly: But "Brothers" wasn't any good.

Gibbs: Was it better than your last essay?

ON FINDING YOUR VOICE

Kelly: You would probably think so.

Gibbs: Who was the second writer you wanted to impress?

Kelly: After Mary Shelley, it was probably Kazuo Ishiguro. You gave me *The Remains of the Day* to read the summer before junior year, and I absolutely loved it. I wanted Mr. Stevens to be a young man so I could fall in love with him, and we could work together at Darlington Hall. Not really, but I couldn't distinguish my love of the novel from my love of the narrator.

Gibbs: And what was the first thing you wrote after you read *The Remains of the Day?*

Kelly: Oh, I tried my hand at a story about a butler who worked in an English manor, of course.

Gibbs: But you didn't abandon Mary Shelley, did you?

Kelly: No. She still looms large in my imagination.

Gibbs: What you're describing is the development of your voice. As you get older, you add more names to the pantheon of writers you worship. By the time you're forty, there will be several dozen writers you try to impress every time you sit down to work, and not just writers, but filmmakers, photographers, architects, musicians. That's how you develop your own voice. You slowly become a unique convergence of your influences. In the convergence of those influences, something original emerges.

Kelly: How do you avoid becoming a schizophrenic pastiche of better writers?

Gibbs: Can you think of a few successful writers who fit that description?

Kelly: Yes.

Gibbs: Would you say their influences are old or new?

Kelly: I never thought about it before. I suppose they're generally ripping off a bunch of new writers.

Gibbs: Yes. The sort of writer who becomes a "schizophrenic pastiche of better writers" isn't borrowing from Homer, Virgil, Ovid, Sappho, Austen, Tolstoy, Dickens, and Milton. He's usually ripping off twentieth century writers like Italo Calvino and Gabriel Garcia Marquez.

Kelly: What does that prove?

Gibbs: To begin with, it is simply far easier to imitate new writers than old ones. Take Calvino. I don't have anything against Calvino. He's quite good. But Calvino's influences were old and his ability to pay homage to them was hard won. I understand how Calvino could be the first writer a thoughtful high schooler fell in love with and wanted to imitate. But Calvino is a relatively recent writer, he didn't come from nowhere, and any young writer with a sturdy intellect will quickly begin to wonder who influenced Calvino. If you really love Calvino, you want to know who his heroes were, so you start digging.

Kelly: If Calvino made you want to write, you want to know who made Calvino want to write.

Gibbs. Yes. When all a writer's influences come from a highly limited historical period, it isn't humility or wonder, but laziness. Anyone who creates schizophrenic pastiche hasn't done much digging. They're not interested in getting a double portion of the master's spirit. They settle for the master's ring. They are content with a few shallow allusions and references to his work that will convince others they have good taste.

Kelly: So, the only way to achieve genuine originality is to not try?

Gibbs: I have suggested that you sit down to write with the goal of pleasing writers who are better than yourself. The only way to achieve genuine originality is to attempt the opposite: a patient, studied, in-born homage to others. Not even Christ Himself attempted a completely original ministry. His ministry was largely patterned after the great prophets in the Old Testament. He wasn't the first to fast for forty days in the wilderness. He wasn't the first to raise the dead. He borrowed his cousin's greatest disciples. Masses came to Him seeking something new and He offered them "the sign of Jonah." Granted, there are numerous events in Christ's life that are without parallel, but one would have a hard time proving from the Gospels that originality is all that important to God.

DIALOGUE 12

On Loopholes

Marcus: Why did you count my paper late?

Gibbs: The paper was due on Friday, and you turned it in on Monday.

Marcus: But I wasn't in class on Friday.

Gibbs: You weren't in my class on Friday, which was the first class of the day; however, you came to school later in the day.

Marcus: How do you know that?

Gibbs: I saw you around school.

Marcus: But I wasn't at school during first period, which is when your class meets, and so I wasn't present to turn in my paper.

Gibbs: Did you have a paper to turn in on Friday?

Marcus: No.

Gibbs: Which is why you didn't bring me the paper on Friday when you arrived late.

Marcus: But if I wasn't in your class to turn it in, why is it marked late?

Gibbs: Because you skipped my class Friday morning just so you would have a plausible-sounding excuse for turning it in Monday.

Marcus: That seems like a legitimate reason to me. Why are you calling it a "plausible-sounding excuse"?

Gibbs: Skipping class to get a few extra days to work on an assignment is not the kind of plan you would present to a teacher prior to the fact, is it?

Marcus: No, but so what?

Gibbs: Why would you not present that plan to a teacher prior to the fact?

Marcus: A teacher might not like it.

Gibbs: Why?

Marcus: Because teachers have to say, "I want you in class," even when it's not true.

ON LOOPHOLES

Gibbs: That's true. But is that the only reason?

Marcus: Did you just admit that teachers have to say that even when it isn't true?

Gibbs: Yes. Are there any other reasons a teacher might not want students skipping class to get extra time on an assignment?

Marcus: I don't know. I'm still too blown away that you admitted teachers have to say, "I want you in class," when it's not true.

Gibbs: Are basic good manners really so mind-blowing?

Marcus: How is it good manners to say, "I want you in class," even when it's not true? That's not good manners. It's a lie.

Gibbs: If a certain student hates class, and does not veil his contempt for class, but actively tries to derail lectures, mocks the comments of fellow students, and insults the teacher after class, it is hardly surprising a teacher would breathe a sigh of relief when that student was out of class. At the same time, teachers are a good bit like judges, police officers, or priests, in that they are custodians of public trust. Because such profound responsibility rests on teachers, they are not free to do and say whatever they like but must submerge certain personal opinions they hold beneath the high calling of their public persona. When a teacher says, "I want you in class," he is speaking from his public persona. It is no more a lie than an officer's badge or a judge's robes.

Marcus: That sounds like an excuse for telling lies.

Gibbs: Given how little respect you have for the public persona of the student, that is not surprising.

Marcus: I don't believe in "the public persona" of the student.

Gibbs: Of course. Very few people do, which is why we no longer dress up for church, why we conduct wedding services wherever we like, why you don't call me "sir," why I don't call my boss "sir," why dinner guests no longer wait for the lady of the house to take the first bite of her meal before beginning themselves. We've been taught to believe that the level of mess, entropy, and informality which comes naturally is honest and therefore virtuous, although none of it has made the world a nicer place to live. You would enjoy class more if you believed in the public persona, though. Your classmates would respect you more, as well.

Marcus: How do you know my classmates don't respect me?

Gibbs: It was your classmates who told me you were skipping my class on Friday morning as an excuse for turning in your paper on Monday.

Marcus: Again, how is that an excuse? Why isn't it a legitimate reason?

Gibbs: As a strategy for getting a few extra days to work on the assignment, there's an appearance of legality to what you did—but it's not the kind of thing you can be proud of, not the kind of thing you could do openly. Rather, it is the kind of thing you were hoping would not be discovered, the kind of thing you know you cannot get away with twice. In other words, it's a loophole.

Marcus: I'm not ashamed of what I did.

Gibbs: That is somewhat true. You told your classmates about it, but not me. Your goal was to look smarter than me, to shame me, and to insult the diligence of your classmates, who got their papers turned in on time.

Marcus: What if my goal was just to get a few extra days to work on the assignment?

Gibbs: You would not have told your classmates about it.

Marcus: What if I told my classmates just so they could see how much I cared about doing a good job?

Gibbs: At this point in the school year, I have no reason to believe that's true.

Marcus: You can't prove that.

Gibbs: And you can't prove your righteous motives, either.

Marcus: I don't have to, though. This whole argument concerns a matter of the heart, a matter of conscience. You don't know for certain what's in my heart, which means you have to believe me when I say I had the best of intentions in skipping your class on Friday.

Gibbs: Fascinating. Please, go on.

Marcus: Christians have to take people at their word. "Give to the one who asks you..." as Jesus says.

Gibbs: Well, we've reached the place in this conversation where I might say something like, "So, do you have to give me everything I ask of you, as well?" and I might try to get you to reason from your own inane premises and gradually defeat your argument. But I've taught a few loophole artists before, and I'm simply not up for debating you. Not even you believe what you're saying, which means that no amount of logic in the world is actually going to shut you down. Suffice it to say, there are enough verses in the Bible about grace, mercy, charity, forgiveness, and good intentions to keep a small-minded man condemning the world for the rest of his life.

Marcus: What's that supposed to mean?

Gibbs: It means my obligation here and now is to be useful to you, to do you some good, and debating you any further on the Christian philosophy of conscience wouldn't help you at all. It would make you twice as dangerous to yourself as you already are. There are times when taking a man seriously means not taking his argument seriously. This is one of those times.

Marcus: So, you're simply not going to give me an answer?

Gibbs: The world is a difficult place to live. Most people live with a staggering number of regrets, secrets, and fears of getting caught or found out. For this reason, real confidence is a genuinely rare thing. It is so rare, in fact, that one rarely finds two people with real confidence in the same room at the same time. Confidence can be used to help others; however, it can also be used to exploit others. Of course, people not only live with regrets and secrets. In our day and age, they also live in a state of perpetual distraction and with a standing list of fifty things they need to do, only twenty of which they can remember at any given time. They forget deadlines. They don't read closely. In such an environment, loopholes proliferate.

Marcus: What exactly do you think a loophole is?

Gibbs: A loophole is simply a confident person using the ambiguity of the English language to exploit a person who lacks confidence. Most people spend their days in the company of people they trust, like family members, friends, coworkers, peers, fellow parishioners. In other words, people who will not try to trick them. Under such conditions, it is easy to forget just how ambiguous many words, phrases, and symbols actually are. When we live with others, we come to define words the same way, interpret phrases the same way, read symbols the same way—and all of this happens organically, accidentally, and invisibly. Because so much of what happens in a certain community is never formally codified and explained, it is easy to surprise others by suddenly taking advantage of how much the community assumes about itself. That surprise is a loophole. Loopholes are never part of a long game, though. They only work short-term.

Marcus: Why is that?

Gibbs: Because people who look for loopholes can't be trusted. You can only burn someone with a loophole once or twice, then they give up on you.

Marcus: Isn't it your responsibility to close off loopholes? Doesn't the existence of loopholes prove that you haven't articulated the rules clearly enough?

Gibbs: No. Wherever you find words, you find loopholes. Loopholes merely prove that anything can be cut in half, including a sentence. Some loopholes are bigger than others, but no law code written by human beings can account for every contingency, every possibility, every technicality. Language works because of shared definitions, shared experiences, and a shared desire to understand others. As someone who talks for a living, I am keenly aware of the fact that just about anything can be misunderstood and misinterpreted— willfully or unwillfully. It is the nature of language to limit and to truncate. Given the expansive nature of the human ego, language will always be potentially, plausibly, and arguably offensive. Speaking is always undertaken as an act of faith which assumes the goodwill of the one listening. But such goodwill can always be exploited.

Marcus: I didn't do anything technically prohibited.

Gibbs: Is this really how you want the student-teacher relationship to work? "Buyer beware"? "Watch your back"? "Should have checked the fine print"?

Marcus: It's not unfair.

Gibbs: And when you someday marry, do you intend on being technically faithful to your wife? If you asked your wife if she had been faithful to you, would you be comforted if she answered, "Technically, yes"?

ON LOOPHOLES

Marcus: You tend to liken everything to marriage.

Gibbs: When you marry, you'll make a number of promises and vows to your wife. Do you want to be the kind of man who seeks loopholes for those promises? Do you want your wife to seek loopholes in the legal obligations she has to you? Do you want to be the kind of father who looks for loopholes in your legal obligations to your daughter?

Marcus: Why would I do that, though?

Gibbs: For the same reason you skipped class on Friday morning: to get something you wanted which couldn't be acquired openly and honestly. Looking for loopholes becomes a kind of sick logic which drives men to loneliness, self-justification, and the cultivation of secret lives which they find more pleasurable than their roles as fathers and husbands.

Marcus: All that just for skipping class on Friday? Doesn't that seem like an overreaction?

Gibbs: Where do you think unhappy adults come from? You don't think miserable adults come from nowhere, do you? It takes a long time to make a truly miserable adult. You've got to start young. Of course, that also means you've got a long time to prevent adults from becoming miserable, which is what I'm trying to do. When I look at someone like you, I have to ask myself what you will be like ten years from now if you have the same warped sense of justice, the same lack of self-awareness, but more time, money, trust, and power on your hands.

Marcus: Look, can't you just let me go with a warning? Can't you just tell me not to skip class on Fridays again? Why does my paper have to be marked late?

Gibbs: If a late grade on a late paper seems too high a price to pay for such a lesson, I doubt a warning will really sing the message home.

Marcus: What do you get out of grading my work lower?

Gibbs: Nothing. Less than nothing. The fact your parents approved your plan of skipping class on Friday morning means they'll want to schedule a meeting with me after they see your late grade. They'll offer the same excuses and accusations you did. I'll have to explain myself again. It'll cost an hour of my time, if not more. I will lose sleep about it, as well, because with each passing year, I get a little closer to telling people like your parents the unvarnished truth about the kind of person they're raising you to be, although I've not quite crossed that threshold yet. In other words, it would be easier now to let you off the hook, but it would be harder in the long run.

Marcus: How would it be harder in the long run?

Gibbs: If I let you off the hook, you would tell all your classmates your plan worked, which would breed contempt in their hearts not only for me but for this school. That sort of contempt would prompt them to look for loopholes, as well. But if I call you out on your foolishness, the students you bragged to about your plan will see that loopholes don't work. They won't come to class skeptical of the lessons I teach, discouraged by the fact that their bumbling, full-witted teacher was outwitted by a student. They won't think of their

ON LOOPHOLES

teachers as people they must outwit. All of which means they are more respectful in class and more receptive to what I teach them. Besides, if I call you out on your sin, I win a little more respect from you, as well.

Marcus: Why should I respect you more for all this?

Gibbs: Ask me that question again in ten years.

A PARLEY WITH YOUTH

DIALOGUE 13

On Secrets

Moriah: I'm in a real bind.

Gibbs: Tell me about it.

Moriah: A friend of mine told me she had a secret she desperately needed to tell someone, but that she wouldn't tell me the secret unless I swore that I wouldn't reveal it to anyone. So, I did. But after hearing the secret, I am very worried about her.

Gibbs: And you're wondering whether it's allowable to break your promise?

Moriah: Yes. What if I swore to God that I wouldn't tell anyone?

Gibbs: I think I know what your friend's secret is.

Moriah: Really?

Gibbs: Is your friend planning on murdering your entire family?

Moriah: What? No!

Gibbs: Because if she were, you would obviously break your promise and not feel bad about it at all.

Moriah: Sure.

Gibbs: You have your answer, then.

Moriah: But that's entirely different.

Gibbs: Not really. The question on the table is whether it's ever allowable to break a foolish promise. You just proved it is.

Moriah: My friend isn't planning on murdering my entire family, but she could still get very hurt. I guess she already is.

Gibbs: Then what's your conundrum?

Moriah: Is it always a sin to break a promise?

Gibbs: Not if making the promise was sinful or keeping the promise is sinful. Promises to sin are not binding.

Moriah: Why not?

Gibbs: Think about the sort of promises that have a functional role in society. When people marry, they take oaths to be faithful to one another, even when it is hard to do so. Before people testify in court, they make promises to speak the truth, even when it is unpleasant or embarrassing to do so. When people join the military, they make promises to defend the Constitution, which is an icon of this nation, even when it means risking their lives to do so. We make promises in order to fight our temptations. We make promises to do good because we know the inclinations to lust, deception, and cowardice are powerful. That's the proper role of a promise. Any promise to sin is antithetical to the very nature of a promise. Promises exist to keep you from sinning.

Moriah: I understand that, although I didn't exactly promise to sin. I just promised not to reveal someone else's sin.

Gibbs: And how many times have you lied in order to keep this sin hidden?

Moriah: Well, once or twice.

Gibbs: Why did your friend tell you this secret?

Moriah: She said she needed to get it off her chest.

Gibbs: Then why make you promise not to tell anyone?

Moriah: So she wouldn't get in trouble.

Gibbs: In other words, she wanted the relief that comes with confession but not the change of heart which comes with repentance.

Moriah: I suppose.

Gibbs: In the future, when someone says, "I have a secret to tell you, but you have to promise not to tell anyone," you ought to reply, "I'm not making that promise, but tell me anyway."

Moriah: But they won't tell the secret.

Gibbs: Actually, they will. People who want to talk can't help themselves.

Moriah: Well, if it ever happens again, I might do that, but it doesn't do me much good now.

Gibbs: For now, you should start by acknowledging the real reason you made the promise not to tell anyone.

Moriah: What's that?

Gibbs: Curiosity. A desire to get some juicy gossip. A desire to be in the know.

Moriah: That's not true at all. I wanted to help her.

Gibbs: You've already lied twice to help keep this secret. Be honest about the kind of help she actually wanted from you.

Moriah: We're friends. We care about each other. You make it all sound so duplicitous.

ON SECRETS

Gibbs: What could possibly be duplicitous about lying for your friends?

Moriah: You know what I mean.

Gibbs: What did your friend mean when she said she needed to "get something off her chest"?

Moriah: The weight of her secret was too great to bear alone.

Gibbs: She wasn't alone with the secret, was she?

Moriah: What do you mean?

Gibbs: The secret almost certainly involves sex or drugs, in which case other people know about it. Her boyfriend, her girlfriend, the guy she's buying coke from, the guy her boyfriend's buying coke from. What your friend wanted was an innocent person to share her secret with, someone who would be impressed with just how adult her problems are, someone who would be flattered she was deemed worthy of holding the secret, someone who would buy the idea she was "going through some difficulties right now."

Moriah: She is going through some difficulties right now.

Gibbs: That's such a gutless, banal way of describing continual capitulation to sin. When your friend told you her secret, did you tell her to stop sinning?

Moriah: What she needed was a shoulder to cry on.

Gibbs: Did you at any point in the conversation tell her what she was doing was wrong?

Moriah: No.

Gibbs: Have you told her since then?

Moriah: No.

Gibbs: Then why come to me?

Moriah: I don't know. I thought maybe you would understand. At times, you seem to remember quite clearly what it's like to be seventeen, although right now you come across as a totally unsympathetic adult.

Gibbs: There are times when I think this school ought to offer a class for teenagers on how to speak to adults. It would be a little like teaching American businessmen how to speak to Saudi oil merchants.

Moriah: What's that mean?

Gibbs: Try to see it from my perspective. You come to me quite troubled about a foolish promise you made to keep a friend's secret. I can either tell you to keep the secret or not keep the secret. What do I stand to lose by telling you not to keep the secret and simply tell your friend's mother?

Moriah: What do you stand to lose by doing that? Nothing.

Gibbs: Right. And what do I stand to lose by telling you to keep the secret?

Moriah: Nothing. You haven't done anything wrong.

Gibbs: Incorrect. If your friend is telling innocent people like you her secrets, her secrets aren't going to last much longer. People are going to find out what she's done, then they're going to find out you knew, then they're going to talk to you and ask you, "Why didn't you tell anyone?" And you'll say, "Well, I asked Mr. Gibbs if I should keep the secret, and he said I should." Then I'm complicit in you and your friend's stupidity, and I have a lot more to lose than you do. If you tell your friend's parents what she's doing, you might lose that friendship. I don't really care all that much about this friendship, especially given what your friend is pulling you into. I have a wife, two kids, and a career on the line, and my career is jeopardized when I tell teenage girls their teenage friendships should have priority over their safety, over potential trips to jail or Planned Parenthood clinics. I was a teenager once. I know that most teenage friendships don't last all that long after graduation. So, forgive my bluntness, but saving this friendship just isn't a concern of mine.

Moriah: That's selfish.

Gibbs: No more so than demanding my children brush their teeth because I can't afford for them to get cavities. It's really just common sense.

Moriah: Is this the way adults make all their decisions about teenagers?

Gibbs: A lot of them, yes. We look at what could go wrong, what is likely to go wrong, who will take responsibility for things when they go wrong, and what can be gained from the risk. Most of the time, teenagers expect adults to take significant legal and financial risks so that they can have fun, but reasonable adults don't place any sort of premium on the importance of teenagers having fun. Children can't get sued. Adults can. And it's the adult parents of injured children who tend to sue at the drop of a hat. Again, reasonable adults keep this sort of thing in mind when teenagers ask for permission to do something dumb and dangerous just so they can have fun. That's basically what being an adult means: anticipating all the ways you could get sued.

Moriah: It sounds like you've already decided what I'm going to do about my secret.

Gibbs: Unless your friend is planning on getting an abortion this afternoon, you should tell her she needs to confess everything to her parents quite soon. You should apologize for making a foolish promise to her, a foolish promise that you will have to break unless she comes clean. When she understands what's on the line, she will almost certainly tell them herself.

Moriah: She'll be mad at me.

Gibbs: Yes, and when you look back on this in fifteen years and understand it all with an adult's perspective, you'll realize how mad at her you should have been at the time.

Moriah: Do you think she'll get over it?

ON SECRETS

Gibbs: It will be something you both have to get over. The sort of things she's likely to say to you this afternoon when you tell her to come clean will probably end whatever trust remains between the two of you. More often than not, it's the person in your place who decides the friendship isn't worth saving.